Dirty Money

How to Earn a Significant Income with Your Service-Based Business and Enjoy a Good Life!

By Chris Phillips,

President & Co-Founder of Send Jim

Dirty Money
How to Earn a Significant Income with Your
Service-Based Business and Enjoy a Good Life!

Published by Phillips Publishing
14165 N Fenton Rd.
Suite 201F
Fenton, MI. 48430

ISBN: 978-1-7325710-0-6

Cover design by Jim Saurbaugh, JS Graphic Design

or any other jurisdiction, is the sole responsibility of the purchaser or reader.

This book is intended to provide accurate information with regards to the subject matter covered. However, the Author and the Publisher accept no responsibility for inaccuracies or omissions, and the Author and Publisher specifically disclaim any liability, loss, or risk, whether personal, financial, or otherwise, that is incurred as a consequence, directly or indirectly, from the use and/or application of any of the contents of this book.

To my wife who loves me better than anyone ever could, to my father who never let me down, and to my business partner, Josh Latimer who inspired me to write this book.

Table of Contents

Foreword

You are not merely holding a book – you're holding a roadmap to greatly accelerate the growth and profitability of your business.

I know, a statement like that might be worthy of a smirk or eye-roll, but bear with me for a couple minutes and, I promise, you'll thank me later!

As an author and business coach, I am frequently asked to review and recommend books. As much as it is an honor to be asked, I have to say no to most requests purely based on my busy schedule. When my friend and client, Chris Phillips, asked if I would review his book, *Dirty Money*, based on how much I admire and respect Chris for what he's accomplished in his life, both personally and professionally, I agreed to take a look and am I ever glad I did.

Having been in business as long as I have, you see far too many so-called "experts" who talk a good game and recite things that they have learned from others. But when you peel the onion back one or two layers, you find out that some "experts" have never actually done what it is they teach others to do.

Chris Phillips is the real deal. He is an "everyman" who has been through hard times, experienced a lot of struggle and pain in his life, as well as his share of failure. All of this and more make him someone you can instantly relate to and want to learn from.

And while Chris's personal story will grab your attention, it's what he's done in business – businesses just like yours – that will have you turning the pages late at night, unable to put this book down, even when you know you have an early day!

Allow me to share a few of the profit nuggets in *Dirty Money* that caught my attention. I won't share the "punch line" and instead leave that for you to discover. However, I encourage you to view the next few lines as an appetizer to the main course that awaits you in the pages of this book.

- Get off the ladder: At first glance, given the audience, I was curious about this one myself! But this lesson alone is worth 100 times the investment you've made to read this book.
- "It's Not about the Dirt": Really?!? Yes, the truth is, as Chris shares, your customers don't care about the PSI – they want a clean deck (or windows, gutters, etc.) and they want the job done right, on time, and for the price quoted.
- You don't get to make bigger deposits based on how hard you've worked.
- Hiring someone to clean is a luxury. If your customers are not referring you left and right – you need to read this section fast.

A dose of reality: There is a statistic that's been around for decades that says 80 percent of small businesses fail within the first five years. Of those that survive – far too many only "exist" and despite hard work, never prosper.

In *Dirty Money*, Chris talks about two types of operators in the cleaning business, one is known as "Clean-Shirt Chris" and the other is "Lord Joe Saint Stink-o-Lot."

I suggest the after reading this book and, more importantly, implementing what you learn, I hope you all choose the smart alternative and become your own version of Clean-Shirt Chris and create more success and freedom for yourself.

Chris Phillips is an everyman, someone who has beaten the odds, weathered many storms, and has created an enviable record of success in business. And I predict that after reading this book and implementing even some of the lessons Chris has used to create one of the most successful cleaning businesses in the industry, you too will be on your way to achieving more growth, profitability and freedom.

Jim Palmer - The Dream Business Coach
www.getjimpalmer.com

Preface:
They're Out to Get You, But...

First, I want to start this book by telling you that I am proud of you for all of your failures! I know you have them because we all do. Have you ever used the phrase "those people" when describing the people who are out to get you? You know the ones I'm talking about. Now it's time to put them in their place and knock them down a notch... and get some dirty money. I know you can do it!

But to your own self be true. Let me enlighten you with a few facts. Your suspicions are accurate. The people who you think are out to get you, well, they are. The people who want you to fail, they do. The people, even in your family, who say you're a bum and will never amount to anything, they are real, but are they right?

Let's call them "the peoples," whether they be family peoples, friends peoples, or stranger peoples, they are out to get you. You see, they need to be right about you because being right keeps them comfortable in their own little world and in their own skin.

Have you ever told a friend or family member about your dream of making it big in business, and all you got back was why it was a stupid idea and that it would never work? I hate that! People can be spirit sucking! The real question that you must ask and answer for yourself is: How badly do you want it?

Entrepreneurial Spirit

Let me start by sharing a story about me that indicated early on that I would never be truly happy working for someone else.

When I was 19, I was quite the partier, and in my hometown of Fenton, Michigan, there are 72 lakes in a 10-mile radius. Summers in Michigan are beautiful. Being on the lake drinking with my friends and lots of pretty women in bikinis was my idea of fun. There was one problem that kept me from the fun: I had a job in a metal shop. It paid me $4.00 an hour, and they "owned" me all summer, six days a week from 6:00 a.m. until 4:00 p.m. It was miserable work – noisy and dirty. I can still smell the propane from the fork lifts.

One beautiful summer weekday, all my friends planned this major bash at the lake, but I couldn't get the day off. I went in that morning just sick that I was going to miss out on the fun. My friends actually drove through the parking lot around my morning break just to rub it in.

I don't know if you've ever felt trapped, but I certainly did that morning and I couldn't stand it. I had to figure out some way to get out of there and get to party land.

Here was my plan. I knew the boss would never fall for me being sick. (You see, I worked for my dad's business partner, so he knew me like a son.) So faking an illness wouldn't work, but what if I were to somehow get injured? They would have to let me go, right? Head trauma was out of the question, but what about a cut? Like a really bad cut that would require me to go for stitches?

I took a box cutter and got up enough courage to do the deed. I actually still have scar from this by the way, and the story gets better. My first attempt didn't get the result I wanted, so I was forced to try it again. Here I was in the back of the shop, carving on my finger, and I looked up to see one of the other workers watching me with horror on his face. He knew exactly what I was doing and why. He'd been outside when all those beautiful girls drove by during break time. He walked over and said, "If you want it that bad, your secret is safe with me." Oh thank God… the plan was still on!

By now, the cut had started to bleed pretty good, and it really hurt after four or five attempts. So I pushed out as much blood as I could and then went running up to the office to launch my plan to freedom. I said, "Oh my God. I cut my finger really bad, and I need to go to the doctor." My boss had stepped out for a bit, and I knew the secretary wouldn't look too closely after seeing all the blood. I remember the sun hitting my face as I exited that hell hole. Freedom at last.

Now all I had to do was get a couple stitches and I would be home free – a valid excuse to leave work and join the fun. When I got home to grab my bathing suit, I took a closer look at my handy work, and wouldn't you know it… it wasn't good enough. I mean I would actually need stitches to get out of this without losing my job and disgracing my father so further action was needed. My dad was a whip in the kitchen and had a set of really nice, really sharp German knives. Here we go again. It took another four to five tries, but finally I felt confident that stitches were needed.

Off to the doctor I went with a great big smile on my face. It took forever! One hour turned into two, but I had to get this done right. Finally, I had them stitch me up… four stitches in all. I had to return home for a minute and to my horror, the boss had left a message on the answering system to call him. By now it was 1:30. So I had to call him back. To my relief, he just wanted to make sure I was okay. By the time I got to the lake, it was after 2:00. I could have simply finished my shift at 4:00 and been at the lake by 4:30… without having to slice my own hand and get four stitches.

I tell you this humiliating story to make a point. I never thought about "going to the lake" once it was my business and I was working for myself. Some people are just wired that way. For me, working for someone else's dreams just doesn't cut it! (Get it?) If you relate to my story in any way, then you are an entrepreneur and have the entrepreneurial spirit. Don't work for someone else, and you'll never have to cut yourself or take any other analogous action to have some fun. The moral of this story is that if you want something bad enough, you will do just about anything to get it.

I am here to tell you that you can do it! If I can make it, you definitely can. And I am proud of you for all the failures you have had throughout your life; it is what makes you you. God made you this way, and you can't help that. But you want to control your own destiny, learn from your failures, write your own story, build your own business, and win, win, win!

So let's knock "the peoples" down off their high horses. Let's sweep the leg. And let's prove them all wrong. You can do it, so let's start now!

Chapter One:
Climbed Down the Ladder and Skyrocketed My Income

You don't often hear people talk about climbing down the ladder of success, but that's exactly what I did. It's also exactly what I hope to help you achieve in the pages of this book.

To start, I feel I need to give you a little bit of my background, so you fully understand that I was exactly like you at one point (perhaps even worse as you might gather from the "knife story") and to share the steps I took to provide you with a road map, so you can follow a similar path to success.

First, I hated working my tail off and making a lot of money... for someone else! I felt that way on numerous occasions before I finally took the plunge to start my own business. I started Phillips Services and knew in my heart and deep down in my gut that I would be wildly successful because I had a great work ethic, and heck, I knew everything there was to know about window cleaning, pressure washing, and gutter cleaning. I knew I could turn all that dirt into real income – dirty money, so to speak.

To me, that was the magic formula that would equal success and a life of financial struggle no more. Seriously, I knew more about PSI, cleaning solutions, and how to get more work done in a 12-hour day than anyone else, so success was almost guaranteed – or so I thought.

Perhaps you're reading this, thinking about starting a service-based business, and you have similar feelings:

Why work hard for someone else? Why not work hard for your own profit? If you're going to work hard, it should lead you to living the life you want and dream about.

Or maybe you currently have such a business and, like me, you've discovered that maybe, just maybe, your former employer or some of your competitors who appear to be killing it might actually know something more about the business you're in than setting an alarm clock, having a strong work ethic, and which power nozzle to use to maximize PSI and blast the dirt from that deck with such force it ends up in the neighbor's yard.

So let me make some bold claims about this book. If you follow the road map laid out here, you will not only explode your business but will also have the time and freedom to enjoy it – aka living the life you want and dream about. Now here is the catch and the hard part: You will need to die to yourself and learn to love people who are hard to love and have a desire to help them. Still with me?

I first want to be very honest with you about who I am and the fact that I have had more failure than most. I struggled with my parents' divorce, followed a year later with my mother's tragic death in a car accident. So by the age of 12, I had started drinking and smoking pot. At 16, I graduated to LSD and cocaine, and by 21, I was a convicted felon for a drug possession for a large quantity of cocaine. After going to jail for 90 days, I never touched hard drugs again. However, I did not put down the booze, and by 34, I almost drank myself to death. In fact, the doctors gave me less than a year to live unless I started making some big changes.

Now don't get me wrong. I had a lot of good things happen to me in my youth, too. I played classical piano, studied for four years at the Interlochen Center for the Arts national music camp, was a chess champion, sailed Hobbie Cats, was an all-state football player and extreme skier, and had many friends and was very popular. However, the reality was that my life was a mess. By 1999, I'd come to the end of myself. It was then that I surrendered to God, and in September 1999, I entered Teen Challenge and spent the next 12 months getting to know Jesus Christ. (Despite its name, Teen Challenge serves both teens and adults.) I graduated from Teen Challenge a year later and felt like I could conquer the world.

I get to tell people that I met my wife in "Greece," but we really met in the musical, *Grease*. We were that couple that could make everyone sick with how in love we were. (I love to tell my love story with my wife but will spare you that here… but ask me about it when you meet me.) Lucky in love… but not business. I had yet to learn that business success takes a lot more than luck and hard work. Even though I had come back from the dead, I still had a ton of bad habits when it came to business.

In 2001, I started Phillips Services, and although I was a hard worker, I didn't understand business and I certainly didn't understand how to **run** a business. So for the next seven years, I really floundered. I was the guy who could do it all but wasn't really very good at any one thing. I did painting, pressure washing, window cleaning, car detailing, mulching, mowing, hardscaping, flat work, and I chopped wood. I literally would do anything for a buck. I even sold frozen food out of the back of a truck for a time. I lost a small fortune in multi-level marketing schemes, and my wife couldn't understand why I wouldn't just go get a job. I had a family to support, after all. So after seven years of trying to do it my way and doing anything for a buck, I went out and got that job. It was a sales job with a $35,000 annual salary plus commission, and I worked for this little guy who was extremely intense and taller than my 6'3" frame… when he stood on his wallet. I knew the first day I arrived that they were recording my every phone call, so I put my head down and I just dialed… and dialed… and dialed.

I was hired with four other people, all of whom were gone within the first two days, so I watched people go in and out of the door while I just hung on for dear life. I was selling thin client (lightweight computers) technology and scanners at a very high margin and absolutely hated my life. It was an hour and a half commute in good weather and an additional hour drive when the weather was bad. I spent 10 hours a day on the phone, and I did really well, but after a year, I was so sick of it, I needed a change.

My office overlooked a beautiful subdivision of houses, and I kept thinking, "If I would just work this hard in my own business washing houses, I could make a small fortune and be a lot happier." So I called my wife and told her I was going to start a pressure washing business. God bless her; she said, "I just want you to be happy." My friends and other family were not so sympathetic. It was 2008 (remember the crash and the economic downturn?) and I finally had a stable job. The comments included: "You are starting a pressure washing job? Is that even a thing? Are you crazy? The economy is a mess. This is the worst time to try this."

Yes, I struggled the first year but was happier than ever, and the following year, I partnered with Josh Latimer to help grow Birds Beware Window Cleaning and Pressure Washing into an entrepreneurial monster. In June 2011, we achieved our first $50,000 month with $52,355. At that point, the doubters – all of those people who told me I was crazy – started calling me "really lucky." Fast forward to May 2015: We sold the business and that month was our highest revenue at $186,000 in residential cleaning.

So what changed? Why was somebody able to achieve such great business success after so many years of failure? I attribute most of it to God, the grace my wife gave me, and of course, it didn't hurt to have a rock star partner. It was hard work and took a lot of grit, but I was never going to give up because going back to that sales job or anything like it was not going to be an option.

Living Proof

The path we took and the systems that we created for Birds Beware Window Cleaning is what this book is about. I know it seems counterintuitive to most small business owners who provide a service, but ***doing less of what your core business is will actually make you more money.*** I'm living proof!

I struggled with this because I loved doing the actual cleaning work. I was really good at it, and people really saw value in what I did every day, so I received a lot of compliments, which, after years of failure, felt really good. I also got a lot of referrals and generated a lot of revenue. I didn't like training people because, for the most part, I felt people needed to be spoon-fed everything. If someone asked, "How can I help?" my thinking was that they were simply in the way. I can't tell you how many times I just said, "Get out of the way. I'll do the rest of the work; you can go sit in the truck." I had a lot of pride in my work and the level of my effort. However, my people skills did not match my work skills.

At this point of our partnership, Josh stopped working in the business and doing the cleaning and on-site work and started to develop systems to make our business run smoother. One day, he told me, "Chris, I want you to get off the ladder. We are going to start calling you 'clean-shirt Chris'." I must admit I was a little pissed off and wondered why he wouldn't again put a dirty shirt on instead and join me to help make a couple grand a day. I struggled with this for about six months, until one day, I almost fell off a roof which would've been career ending if it didn't kill me.

That incident really got me thinking about what I was actually doing. I was self-employed and one fall or serious injury away from being totally out of business. My pride was getting in the way of allowing the company to grow. It was that day that I decided to stop doing the grunt work if it all possible. I went to work being the best sales person I possibly could with a clean shirt, and I surrendered the grunt work to the $12- and $15-an-hour guys.

Lightbulb!

I had been doing $15-an-hour work, but when I got off the ladder and went out in the sales role, I was making the company $500 to $1000 an hour by closing large accounts and setting up work for multiple crews. As the business started to explode, I found myself getting into another prideful habit. I started to think that no one could sell as well as I could. I was the reason all these accounts were happening, and I got comfortable in my sales job. Another lesson learned: You can hire a sales person to do what you do in the same way you can hire someone to do the $15-an-hour work.

> *You need to get out of your own way and possibly "out of your own business" to generate more success. In other words, get off the ladder.*

I'll guess that at this point, you may be thinking, "Well, if you don't do the work and you don't do the sales, what do you do? Office work?" Nope. That can be hired, too.

You may not believe it now, but your business can run just as well if not better without you. This book is about the steps you need to take to get you out of your business and out of the way of your own success.

The Secret to Success

Here is the secret of success in this business, and you only have to do it once. You need you create a written blueprint for everything that relates to your business and its success. This needs to have a start and end date. You need to know where you are going and what that journey will look like. Leave no stone uncovered. The better, more detailed, and deeper you go in this effort will directly affect the size of your wallet and bank account. And last but not least, have a reason to complete it. Why do you want to put in the effort? Why do you want to run your own successful business? What does your dream lifestyle look like? Take time to answer those questions honestly and directly and get a mental image (or even a physical one) of your dream lifestyle – bigger house, vacation property, early retirement, etc. Once you have that worked out, the rest is easy.

I can and will tell you that the process can be very challenging without the help of a coach or mentor to hold you accountable, to ask the tough questions, to guide you through rough waters, and to keep you on track.

So how does all of this work? Remember that I told you I found it hard to work with others? I am impatient and, when I am working, I just want to get the job done as fast as possible and go home. In my mind, the concept that "time is money" certainly rang true and was a guiding principle. Let me tell you a story about a guy I called Dangerous Dave. Now let's get this straight: Dave is an awesome guy and I came to really love the guy. He was a total blessing to our business, and customers absolutely loved him. Dave's first job with me was a house wash, and we were down streaming SH (pool shock). I said, "The only thing that *can't* happen today is that this bucket gets knocked over."

So I start pressure washing and not three minutes later, here comes Dave, running toward me, ghostly white and I said, "You knocked the bucket over didn't you?"

Yep, true story. Dave also had a very hard time with ladders. In fact, he fell twice. So it would be fair to say Dave needed to work for someone else or possibly in another business, but the fact is that *I was the problem*. I assumed that people would understand ladder safety and a simple thing like knocking over pool shock on people's grass would be very damaging, but I never took the time to train him properly.

I share that story to underscore the importance of training. The investment of time, training, and inspiration into people's lives never comes back void. I have seen ten times the return back to me without fail now that I have learned the importance of those investments.

> *Hands down, your investment in employee training will always return a positive ROI!*

In this business, it is so important to make sure you have a written manual on all procedures from A to Z. Your employees need to go through a full training program, and yes, they need to be tested on your procedures before you send them out into the world to do the actual work. I let Dave down and, in the end, lost a great guy and a great employee who my customers loved.

Take time to note right now that if you like being self-employed but you don't work well with others, the rest of this book will not help you. However, if you want to grow something special that works for you and can provide you with a significant income and the freedom to enjoy to it, then roll up your sleeves and let's get started.

Working Smarter, Not Harder

- Success in this business lies in learning to love people who may be hard to love and be dedicated to helping them.
- Hard work is not the answer. While a solid work ethic is an admirable trait, you'll have to learn to work smarter rather than harder in order to achieve the success and life you want.
- Don't get stuck in a rut doing the hourly rate labor. Your talent will serve you better when used elsewhere.
- You can hire for everything from production to office work to sales.
- Get out of your business and out of your own way to be successful.
- While you can hire for any job function, training and your ability to work with and get along with others is critical.

By working smarter rather than harder, you will be more like Clean-Shirt Chris and far less like ol' Stink-a-Lot!

Chapter Two:
It's Not about the Dirt

So many of us cleaning artisans believe that what sets us apart from our competition is knowing and talking about all of the technical aspects of what we do. However, I'll let you in on a secret: Your customers do not care about the GPM, the PSI, the pH or anything and everything else that has fancy letters or is wrapped up in the jargon of the business. It's not about the dirt; it's about understanding and exceeding your customers' expectations. They want results, and when you can go above and beyond the results they expect, you are on the right path.

Now look, before all you techies out there who love the jargon and specifics get to hating on me for what I just suggested, please understand I love great equipment and I love to talk war stories as much as you do, but unless you are doing work for an engineer or a client with the same level of technical appreciation, don't waste your time... or theirs.

Focus your attention on the relationships, and that means taking the focus off of you and putting it on your customer. People, for the most part, love to be heard. Before you roll your eyes, taking those 15 extra minutes to listen to someone's problem may seem like a waste of time, but it is not. (I do draw the line at gossip, however.) This is time spent building a relationship, and relationships are the foundation you need to be successful.

Equip yourself with great questions that will help you know how to best serve your customer. Questions like, "Have you ever had this service done before? What did you like best? Was there something you didn't like? What's important to you?"

There will be customers who don't want to talk. They may be of the mindset that they've hired you to do a job, so do it. You really need to mirror your customer and figure out what they need and *want*.

> *Your customers don't really care about how you get it clean; they just want it clean!*

So if it's about understanding our customer, let's define that. Are you the discount service company on the block that brags about lowest prices? If you are, I'm going to tell you right now: You need to rethink that. Service companies provide what we call a luxury service, and as a luxury service, our customers demand to be pampered and served at a high level. Keep in mind that you are providing a service that customers, if they choose to do so, could probably do themselves. The ones who do choose to do their own cleaning, window washing, gutter or pool cleaning, or whatever service you offer are not the customers you want to pursue. You probably already know that your best clients hire you because they can afford to pay for the service that they have neither the time nor the inclination to do.

These prospects and customers tend to have expensive tastes. So you need to look the part. You need to be clean cut, you need to wear a uniform, you need to have a name tag with a photo ID on it, and your trucks must be clean! You're a cleaning service for goodness sakes, so you first and foremost have to be clean! And don't be smoking at the end of their driveway ever!

> ***Look the part or leave a very bad first impression.***

I really hope I'm preaching to the choir here and that you just read that paragraph and are nodding your head, thinking, "Of course that's how I operate," but I feel like I need to cover this before we get into the deeper stuff. You provide a luxury, not a necessity. Your clients have an expectation not only of the service they receive but how you present that service in the appearance of you and your staff. It all goes hand in hand, and while you may deliver the best end result, how you deliver it and the way you and your staff look while on the job really do matter.

Customer Communication

My new business is named SendJim, and all I do all day is call on small service companies. While I was launching this business and getting it off the ground, I called and talked to thousands of companies. You may be surprised to hear that less than 10 percent of the companies I call ever answer their phones. It always goes to voicemail. Now if I'm a potential customer, what do I do if I get a voicemail? I'm calling the next person on the list that I found in an internet search. You must answer your phone, and if you're too busy, you need to hire somebody to do it whether that be an office manager or a service that answers the phone with the real person. Voice mail, although possibly expected in this day and age due to its proliferation, does not make a good first impression. It might not make a horrible impression since people are practically conditioned to expect it, but I guarantee you that a live voice answering the phone makes a great impression and starts the whole process off on the right foot! With Birds Beware, we would have already delivered the estimate and booked the job before the competition even got back to the customer… usually because the competition was relying on voice mail.

Communication with the customer is also very important. You should always introduce yourself by name, clarify and explain the procedure, and what work will be done. You should ask for permission to get started or to enter the house. At the halfway point, you should ask the customer, "How are things going? Do you have any questions or concerns?"

This is also the best time to point out your upsell opportunities. Never try to sell; always say, "I noticed" or "I recommend." And never make the crew who does the upsell for you do the work *that day*. Think about it: If you've promised your wife that you'll be home at 6 o'clock and you're on time but you noticed the client's gutters need to be cleaned and it will take two more hours, are you ever going to say, "I noticed that the gutters are full and I recommend that we clean them out today?" By letting your crew off the hook of doing the work that day, you will get 100 percent more upsells from them. They will be far more interested in additional work on a schedule rather than creating a last-minute overtime scenario. Yes, with this approach, you might have to do some touch up work, but trust me... this is a real revenue booster for you. ***Upsells are the most profitable sales you can make! Period.***

At the end of the job, you need to offer a walk around with the customer and at that time explain any problem areas or concerns that you discovered. You also need to explain that callbacks are the most costly thing your company experiences because of tight scheduling, so ask the customer to please look carefully and point out any mistakes or problems while you are there, so you can correct them now. By saying this, even if they find something wrong with your work after you're gone, they will be less likely to call you because you gave them the opportunity to point it out while you were there.

> *Go above and beyond on every job, and you will put more money in your bank account every time.*

At the end of the job, you should do something special for your customer, and it can be a simple gesture. We used to have our crew leaders say to the customer, "Hey, you've got a couple strong guys here, do you need anything you have moved?" Now, nine out of ten times you won't be moving a thing. But people don't forget random acts of kindness like that, and if you do end up moving something, you're probably going to get a tip. Get creative.

Maybe leave a small gift or token that ties into your business as a show of your appreciation. The goal is to go above and beyond, and do something that is unexpected, so they remember you and refer you.

Be Persistent and Get More Referrals

Referrals are the best way to grow your business, but you have to ask for them multiple times. At Birds Beware Window Cleaning and Pressure Washing, we would ask new customers *five times* for referrals. All we would say was, "We are a small family business and we really rely on you to refer us to your friends and family, so if we do a good job, please remember us."

This was done at the first contact when they called the office manager. At the end of the conversation, he would close the conversation with the prompt for referrals. The sales rep would say that the same thing at the end of his appointment. The crew leader would say this midway through the job when he was asking if everything looked okay up to that point. The thank-you card we mailed included a similar sentiment, and when we called three days later to ask how the guys did, we asked the same thing.

> *Being persistent and consistent pays off every time!*

You may think this is overkill, but it is very similar, if not identical, to what advertisers know about being consistent and persistent. Most people don't remember a product or service unless they've heard the message about six or seven times. Your customer will remember you based on your stellar service, but they may not remember to refer you. Trust me on this – it works really well.

That said, you need to be very good at what you do, and the work and the end result you deliver to the customer do count, but most important are the relationships that you make and how you nurture them. Our customers became our friends, and with that, they became our cheerleaders and influencers for our business to grow. In the early days, we would hand write our thank-you cards, but by our second year in business, we were doing 150 to 200 jobs a month, so it became too much and we automated that process.

During our second year in business, I realized how important customer follow-up was. The previous year, I had done a house wash for a customer, and the following spring, I gave them a call to see if they would like it done again. To my surprise, the customer said, "Thank goodness you called me! I couldn't remember your company's name." (That was also an important lesson in the need for persistent and consistent requests for referrals. We'd done a great job, but the customer did not remember our name. I'm willing to bet that if we'd been asking for referrals with every contact, that customer would have remembered us!)

I personally remembered everything about that particular job from how she paid to her dog's name, but she was about to call somebody else… and not because we didn't do a good job! It is extremely important to follow up with your customer at least every quarter and remind them of all the services that you offer and perform. This can be done with a letter or postcard. Even an email is better than nothing. Look for ways to make your customers feel appreciated, send them a thank-you message around Thanksgiving, thanking them for their business.

These random acts of kindness need to be done for both customers and employees. With new customers, send them a small gift and at the same time ask for referrals. There is a law of reciprocity that goes on in your customer's head, and they are 100 percent more likely to refer you to their friends and family if you give them a small gift. When you're really small, you can do something like baking a couple batches of cookies and taking them to your favorite customers. Get really creative! As you grow, automate the process. This is the fun hospitality side of the business and will help you grow a business with a great company culture. So remember: It's not about the dirt; it's about the relationships you plant, cultivate, and grow.

Love What You Do

I love what I do now, but one of my first loves was skiing. That's also one of my best childhood memories – annual family trips to Steamboat Springs, Colorado at Christmas and spring break. I first went there in 1970 at age five. At that time, kids skied for free and an adult lift ticket was a whopping $7.00. (Those times have definitely changed!) We stayed right on the mountain in a beautiful condo, and we could ski out the door and right to the lift. For 14 years, I never missed the trip.

Now, I'd been good at many things, but skiing was what I excelled at the most. I could do all kinds of tricks, from flips to helicopters. You name it, I could do it. Big air was my favorite, and I loved showing off, jumping off various rocks, skiing under the lift line, so people could watch and root for me from the chair lift.

I made friends with the locals, and when I was 13, I connected with this cool guy, Jack Taylor... aka "Jumpin' Jack Taylor" who was a three-time world mogul champ. He was skiing with two friends who were on the Women's U.S. Olympic team. At that time, the only way to get to the triple black diamond runs (also known as avalanche shoots in Steamboat Springs), was to take off your skis and hike up. So we did and it was incredible. Here I was skiing with some of the best skier in the world! My heart was racing and the grade was about 75 percent. I'm following the gorgeous Olympic skier down this insane rune, and after we made it out of the steepest part, we were in the trees. I followed her around a big rock and heard her cry out... then thud. We both fell into a tree pit. She started to cry, and I went into rescue mode, assuring her I would get us out of there. I can tell you, it's much harder than you might think to get out of a 10-foot hole under a massive pine tree. The snow was so light, that I couldn't get a good footing. After about 30 minutes, I got out and used one of my skis to pull her out. My reward was an innocent hug and a peck on the cheek. What a great day!

Another great day happened a few years earlier when, skiing with my dad, we witnessed a terrible fall. The woman went ass over apple cart, and wanting to be the hero, I skied over to make sure she was okay. She was a very attractive lady and in a very proper voice informed me that she was okay. I skied off. My dad also skied over to check on her… and realized who she was – Jackie Kennedy Onassis. Her comment to my dad was, "Wow. Your little girl is quite the skier." When my dad told me who she was and what she said, I'd didn't care and didn't think she could be that smart if she mistook me for a girl!

I have so many great memories, and when I think back, I wish I would have pursued the things I loved in my youth to a greater degree. But I do love running my business and am passionate about it. Doing what you love is something only found by a lucky few. I love having my own business… creating my own destiny and being the captain of my own ship. Being able to work outside, face new challenges, and solve new problems every day makes me feel alive! Meeting new people and helping employees achieve their own dreams may not be as glorious as skiing, but it is what I love. I get up every morning and face the day with a smile on my face!

If you feel the same way about your business, count your blessings. Very few have it as good as you. If you find yourself struggling, keep reading because I am passionate about helping you learn to work smarter, not harder and start to climb down the ladder of success the way I did.

Working Smarter, Not Harder

- In every industry, business success is created by developing relationships more than selling a product or service.
- Remember: You are providing a luxury, so your customers expect to be pampered and offered very high-level service.

- Good communication starts with answering the phone. A live voice trumps voice mail every time.
- You need to be consistent and persistent when asking for referrals or you won't get that many.
- You also need to be consistent with your follow-up communications. Stay in touch with your customer to stay top of mind with them, or they are likely to forget you no matter how great the service was that you provided!

By working smarter rather than harder, you will be more like Clean-Shirt Chris and far less like ol' Stink-a-Lot!

It's Not About the Dirt

Chapter Three:
From "You" to "Crew"

Growing up, you probably heard the mantra, "Money doesn't grow on trees" repeated. I sure did. However, I want you to start changing your perspective about that.

I want you to imagine planting, nurturing, and growing a money tree. That is how you need to look at your business. Your business is your money tree. Prune and cultivate it to suit your dreams!

If you're shaking your head, stuck in the mindset that money doesn't grow, let me assure you that I never thought that was possible either. I actually had so many self-limiting beliefs about money and how to go about making and growing it when I first started my business. In fact, my thinking was so limited that I remember saying to my wife, "If I can just make $500 a week, we will be okay." On the first house wash I completed, I made $400 in cash. My wife was waiting for me at the door, and as I got out of the van, I threw the cash up in the air and $20 bills went everywhere. I said, "Honey, it works. I really love doing the physical work... and look at all this money!"

I was outside in the sunshine and actually doing the work was like doing a 12-hour workout every day. I could eat whatever I wanted and not gain weight. I just loved it. But like anything else, after you do it long enough, it kind of loses its charm... and you realize that you're only as good as your next job. I also began to be plagued by the worry about an injury: "What if I fall and get hurt and can't work? I'm really out of business." I remember a friend telling me once that I didn't "have a business" but rather I was "merely self-employed." I remember feeling hurt by that comment but after thinking about it for a while, I realized he was absolutely right. Plus, my initial belief that making $500 a week would suffice was wearing very thin. I wanted more for me... and my family. I realized that I would never break out of that, and what I could achieve as a solo operation would be limited by how many hours I could work doing the actual labor. While I was willing to work 12-hour days, those 60-hour or more weeks did not leave me much, if any, time for my family and to enjoy my life.

Making the Switch

So how do you go from being a one-man band who's running the whole show from sales to doing the work to invoicing and marketing to being totally out of your business? It starts off with knowing your "why."

Talk to about a dozen graduating high school students and ask them what they are going to do with their lives. You might be surprised to find that most of them have no idea what they want to do. If you are lucky, you will find one student who can tell you exactly what they plan to do with their life. Out of those dozen, who is more likely to succeed? Sure, they might all turn out to be very successful... someday. But I think you'll agree that the one with the clear plan will be on the faster path to success.

There is a reason that people who can visualize their destiny tend to achieve it, and then there are those of us who go through life with a reactionary mindset and never amount to much. These are the people who simply take what comes their way without envisioning a better life.

They react to circumstances and events and believe that that's what life entails. Their lives simply "happen," or perhaps you've heard people use the phrase, "But then life got in the way."

Don't let your life simply happen to you or "get in the way" because, if no one has ever told you, you deserve better! I was one of those people who did let life "happen" to me for over 30 years. Granted I did that with a great attitude but without direction and a purpose. The result? I never achieved anything of great significance. For me, at 42-years-old, my "why" became more of what I did not want, which was "that miserable sales job and answering to someone else."

That gave me enough focus to know that my "why" was never going back – never again sitting at a desk making phone call after phone call for something about which I had no real passion and for which my efforts made someone other than myself very rich.

So what is your "why?" With or without one, life goes on, but know that what you desire gives you a chance to map out your dreams.

Stop letting the tail wag the dog. Take control of your life, start each day with a purpose, and know the end of your story. Honestly, I want you to stop reading for a few minutes (if you don't already know your "why") and think about what your personal "why" is… and it cannot simply be to make more money or be successful. Determine your end goal: What will more money or success provide to you and to your family?

With that type of mindset, your destiny is higher than you can imagine. While I've digressed a bit about this topic, I did so because determining your "why" is the foundation for everything else you will learn in this book and be able to employ to enjoy a good life. That said, let's get back to getting you out from underneath your business (off the ladder, out of the truck, etc.) to getting you on top of your business and making it serves you rather than the other way around. Do you have the toughness and grit it takes? I bet you do.

> *You have to switch from "you" to "crew" or you will forever be working in your business with no chance to work on your business to grow and prosper.*

Getting out from underneath your business is no easy task; however, once you understand why you're doing it and you make the decision to never quit, then you have a chance. This is exactly why defining and determining your "why" is so important!

Getting from only *you* to having a crew or crews doing the work is done in four stages. We will cover small working parts and how you can create systems later in the book, but here I want you to understand the process and the transformation that will need to take place.

Stink-a-Lot to Clean Shirt

I want to introduce you to an old friend of mine, "Joe Saint Stink-a-Lot. His name is Joe because he is "your average Joe." His middle name is Saint because he is trying to run his business alone, and he is only doing it to provide for his family. Consider his typical comments to his family, "Why are you mad that I am never here? Don't you know I am doing this all for you." It's often met with, "Nobody asked you to go down this road. Why can't you have a normal job like everyone else?"

His last name is "Stink-a-Lot" because he simply smells bad from working outside in the heat all day. There's also that nervous sweat from worrying about the bills, the next job, and let's face it… life can feel very lonely and just stink a lot when you are starting a business. (According to Bloomberg, eight out of ten entrepreneurs who start businesses fail within the first 18 months. A whopping 80 percent crash and burn.)

Can you relate to Joe? Maybe you are him right now, and if you are, I want to congratulate you on really following the only choice you had – working for yourself. You see, I could fake it for about a year working for someone else, but it was a miserable existence. If you're like me, you can't help it because God just made you this way. Most people don't understand you. They ask, "Why don't you just get a real job?" My advice is never to argue with people that say this. They will never understand.

I want to share some thoughts from my partner, Josh Latimer who came up with the concept of the entrepreneurial birthright: It starts when you have an idea but no one cares. You build a plan, and no one helps; you take massive risk; you're alone; you work and grind for a year and no one sees it. You fail and people expected it; you continue forward, and they smirk; you fail again, and they pity you; you continue forward and struggle, and they laugh. You start winning, and now they try to align themselves with you. You achieve greatness, and they say they know you.

And after all the sweat, the fear, the struggle, they say, "Look how lucky he is!" Man, I love that. The journey of life is what counts... the everyday drudgery that we all go through. Learn to be happy here and now, and you will always have peace. The mountain top is a lonely place where nothing grows, and you can't stay up there for very long or you will die.

History is littered with stories like this. And if you relate to it, you are an entrepreneur. And I congratulate you for it.

I've shared this because I want you to join the 20 percent club of successful business owners rather than being another failed dream. How do you do it? The key is knowing that you don't have to do it alone. Align yourself with like-minded people. Investigate their journeys, copy what worked for them. This struggle is common to everyone who starts a business, but it is people like you and like me that don't settle for the "real job" and go out to create their own destinies. Once you finally make it, you will hear people call you "lucky" or say things like, "Man, I thought of that years ago." Great ideas are worthless without a person with the determination and grit to see it through.

In my life, it wasn't until I surrounded myself with people that were cut from this cloth that I started to succeed win. However, I didn't approach them with an attitude of looking for what they could do for me. Instead, I made a commitment to invest in those relationships, and the commitment was to seek out a way to bring a ton of value to the relationship I was pursuing. This is a learned skill, so start small. You can't just go to an industry leader, a wildly successful entrepreneur or the president of the United States and say, "Here I am. How can I help?" You need to start with the people God has placed in your life today, and this can be humbling and hard. The first year at Birds Beware I worked more than Josh. I bought into his business and I took 1/3 or $.33 on the dollar just to be able to be a part of something that I knew was going to be great.

So get humble, make the hard choices, and seek out people who can show you the way. You can't be the smartest person in the room and expect to grow. There are all kinds of mastermind groups available, and you can invest in your training and pay for a great mentor. All high achievers have a coach or an accountability partner, and they are continually growing. A business partner may not be the answer. When two partners are a lot alike, one of them isn't needed.

Yes, before I was the president and co-founder of Send Jim and before I helped built and sell Birds Beware Window Cleaning, I was Joe Saint Stink-a-Lot... and man did I stink! I've been there, so I want to help you avoid being that guy or move beyond him if you see yourself in that role right now.

Stage 1: Changing Your Role

Let me re-introduce you to "Lord Joe Saint Stink-o-Lot."

- "Lord": Knighted in his own ego of awesomeness.
- "Joe": Down-to-earth, lovable guy (Not too smart but can lift heavy things).
- "Saint": *But I'm doing all* of this for you – my love and family.
- "Stink-o-Lot": Life stinks because you have no time; *you* stink because, well, you just smell bad from working all day, and then add the nervous sweat of trying to close the next job. And it really stinks when you add up all the time you spend doing everything and only making $10 to $20 an hour!

Now let's be real. I know a lot of you are going to say, "Hey, I make $100 an hour!" And maybe some of you do, but I want you to really add up all the time you spend doing jobs that you could pay someone else $12 an hour to do. So Mr. $100-an-hour, why? Why do you continue in the roll of "Lord Joe Saint Stink-o-Lot"?

You really need to humble yourself here if you find that this is where you are truly stuck. Be very honest with yourself. A lot of the time, we take that saint stuff too far, and besides, no one asked you to be a martyr.

When you are at this stage of your business, you do everything as I mentioned earlier. In addition to the actual work, there are all of the "back office" tasks that are needed from accounting to getting supplies to selling to keeping work flowing in the pipeline. I remember thinking about how awesome I was at first because I was tackling everything. (Yes, I was very stuck in my own awesomeness.) Yes, I had a great attitude, and as things came on my plate, "Boom" – I would blast them off!

I did the work, I did the selling and marketing (two separate things, by the way), I managed the oil changes, call backs, ordering new equipment, repairing old equipment, and it goes on and on! The only thing I didn't do was the accounting. So you get the point. I understand that a lot of people are happy here – running the business by themselves doing everything; however, as it was painfully pointed out to me, this is not a business; it is just self-employment. If you get sick or become injured, you are out of luck in a heartbeat. Plus, when do you get to take a day off, let alone a full-blown vacation?

As my business started to grow, I found that I went on this constant roller coaster ride: No work? Go out and sell. Get work; do work. No work? Go out and sell. Get work; do work… and over and over and up and down and up and down it goes. Plus, when you haven't any work, you are much more likely to say yes to things you don't do and don't want to do. "Hey, do you get rid of skunks?" And Stink-o-Lot jumps at the chance to earn a buck and says, "Oh yes, of course I do!" Then you are left wasting time trying to figure out what tools you need and how do you finish it… without adding even more stink!

So your first step in this stage is to hire someone who can replace you. And you're going to need to pour into this person everything you know. You're going to have to let them fail at things on their own at times and as they grow into this role. This is the point at which you can really start developing the dream of what your company is going to look like in one to three years. Share your vision with your new employee, explain to them how they fit in, sell them on the dream, and get them drinking the "Kool-Aid" (aka your "company culture").

Once your assistant has been trained, it's now time to sell. I want to caution you here that whatever you do, don't go out and hire a bunch of people and think that the work is just going to come in. The reality is that it works the other way around. The only way to get out of the "Lord Joe Saint Stink-o-Lot" role is to sell your way out.

The reason why I never got out from under my first business and out of the "Lord Joe Saint Stink-o-Lot" role wasn't because I didn't work hard. It was because I was so unorganized. Couple disorganization with my unwillingness to put in the extra hour doing the things I hated, like building systems to make the work flow better and more efficiently.

Here is the secret: Once I realized I just had to buckle down and work on creating those systems for a short period of time and not forever, it changed my life. The good news is that you don't need to reinvent the wheel or build something from scratch. Instead, seek out a mentor or coach who can show you what they did and how they did it and copy that. (The systems I developed and use successfully are what I teach in my three-month mastermind class.)

I simply want to outline the reason *why* you need them. I hated working on systems because they take a lot of time, and once you've completed them, it is just the beginning of implementing them.

Letting go of being "Mr. Everything" can feel very uncomfortable, but for goodness sakes, just do it! If you continue to be "Mr. (or Ms.) Everything," your business will never grow. It will be impossible for you to achieve significant income and enjoy a good life.

It is a strange feeling the first time you leave the guys on the job to finish without you. The first time I did it, I felt very guilty and after about 30 minutes, the guilt turned to fear. So I drove as fast as I could all the way back to the job site, only to discover that they had already finished and the customer had paid and was happy. If you are like me, once you take this leap and move from "you" to "crew," you won't ever want to do the work again... unless you want to lose some weight!

Stage 2: Changing Your Shirt

Once you get the work in place and hire the person to replace you and a crew, then you can start having fun wearing a clean shirt. Let's call this guy "Clean-shirt Chris." I absolutely love this part of the game. It's the point at which you can really get a lot of swag in your step and the phone starts ringing off the hook, and you're running estimates and raising prices and breaking hearts and taking names. It's a great feeling to be out there filling up your business and burying the workers with more work than they can handle.

Now you're still wearing multiple hats, but at this point, you can start to look at and plan out simple systems. Before, your shirt and sneakers stunk and you didn't have enough time to even think about systems and processes, but here is where you can start to plug other people into doing the $12-hour jobs. So you're still working your butt off, but at least your feet don't stink and you get to wear a clean shirt every day!

However, as I mentioned, I found myself getting into bad habits as "Clean-shirt Chris." For a short time, I stopped motivating the workers. The company culture doesn't develop and arrive just because you don't stink anymore. At this point of the business, we started to develop a file on each employee. I learned their spouse's name, their kids' names, what their "why" was, what they did in their spare time. Once I turned things around and got out of my bad habits regarding my approach to people, "Clean-shirt Chris" really worked hard on building close relationships with our employees. We were a seasonal business, and getting guys to go on unemployment for four month a year was tough, so at Christmas, we went over the top. One year, we took everyone and their families to Frankenmuth, Michigan, and we stayed for two nights at the Bavarian Inn. My kids call it "the castle" because it was awesome with five indoor pools and an indoor putt putt golf course. Yes, this $7,000-plus expense was a lot, but we had a ton of fun, and everyone came back that following spring. It was money invested in not having to hire and train new employees – a function that probably would have cost us more than our investment in a fun weekend. More importantly, it underscored our company culture and reflected how much we really did care about the people who worked for us. And yes, everyone also received a Christmas bonus, so always be sure to budget for that.

Stage 3: The Bad Guy

The next rung down the ladder of success is what I call the "bad guy." The reason you're the bad guy is because when your workers come back from a hard day and you're sitting in an air-conditioned office drinking a pop, you become the bad guy in their eyes. They wonder what the hell **you've** done all day...? (Perhaps when you've worked for someone else, you had the same impression of the boss or management.)

But this is the most important part of the business if you are going to be able to have the ability to have the business run on its own, leaving you with more time and truly being an entrepreneur rather than simply someone who is self-employed.

This is where we systemized what we called random acts of kindness for our employees. I shared with you how I kept a file on every employee. We really went into detail and made certain we knew their spouses' and kids' names and what they liked. In June, when the guys would work 10- to 12-hour days in our really busy season, we would send the wife a gift card for a massage or pedicure or get the whole family movie passes. If you are like me, this is the best part of having your own business. I love to be in the position in which I can bless other people. When I worked by myself, not only did I not earn this kind of money to spend on others, I didn't have the people to give it to.

In our second year, Josh and I told everyone that we had a huge job that would require working the entire weekend, starting early on Friday morning so that we could finish by Sunday evening. In reality, the whole thing was a ruse. We departed in a caravan, but instead of going to the job site, we drove to a beautiful state park where we had a big barbeque waiting. We made everyone take a walk through the forest, so we could talk and then gave everyone the rest of the day (and of course, the weekend) off along with a $100 bonus. That is the type of stuff I live for, and it really boosts employee morale.

I always wanted to stay ahead of employee resentment and diminishing the boss as "the bad guy." We had an open system, so the crew leaders knew to the penny what they were bringing in each week. Running the business with this much transparency may seem much too "open book," but if you let this get away from you, you will wish you were just "the bad guy." If it does get away from you and you fail to be at least somewhat transparent, you can become the scumbag who is ripping everyone off... not just "the bad guy."

> *You're the boss, but you should also take steps not to be the "bad guy."*

When you set up your business with an open book, there is a chance for resentments to develop, so you need to help your workers understand how the money works and where it goes. They need to understand how much it costs to outfit a truck and get and keep it on the road. They need to have a sense of insurance, marketing, and equipment expenses, etc. Some companies do not use a transparent model and keep the money separate to avoid this; however, we really wanted to empower our workers and didn't expect them to be with us forever. We let them know that if they ever wanted to start their own business, we would help them. Some actually took us up on the offer and did well. Others had some resentment but learned the hard way that it isn't just about cleaning the glass. If you choose to be transparent, you'll have to teach your crew what it really takes to run a successful business.

I can't emphasize this enough! Stay connected with your crew leaders and cut out anyone with a negative attitude. In our third year, we had to let our best window cleaner go. Not because he wasn't awesome when it came to customer relations or the fact the he was part of our most profitable crew. The problem was that the way he talked with the other employees was so toxic, we had to cut him out and it really hurt. However, we also knew that leaving him in place could damage our relationship with other employees and also damage the culture we were working very hard to create. In similar vein, don't hire friends or family if you can help it or unless you truly know their work ethic and that they will be an ideal fit in your company and culture. Otherwise with their termination, you will possibly have to say good-bye to a friend or accept tolerating less than enjoyable future family gatherings and holidays.

The "bad guy" always gets a bad rap, and I hated that. However, I am telling you that setting up systems alleviates this. The systems needed for your business to run without you need to be well thought out and incredibly detailed. This is critical, and it is the place where most entrepreneurs need the most help. Admittedly, Josh and I figured out our systems by trial and error. If we had used a coach or mentor, we would have enjoyed success much faster and with less work. (This is certainly an area in which I can help you, if you need it. Some people are extremely organized and love to work on the details, but if this doesn't describe you, I encourage you to reach out to me, using the contact information in the Resource section.)

When the crew returned from a hot day and I'd been in air conditioning, I actually wouldn't have minded trading places. If you are like me in that regard, you just need to push through. I placed a picture of my family on my computer to remind me what I was doing this for and put together a reward for when it was done. (For my reward: a week-long vacation on Mackinaw Island with the family.)

Here is some good news: The systems we can build can be tailored and incorporated into your business, and using the same systems we created will save you years of trial and error, propelling you to success faster. (I recommend that you watch the video links that are included in the Resource section. Yes, there are many ways to build great systems, but I caution you to ensure you are getting advice from someone who has done it successfully.)

That said, don't think just because you have watched the videos and created the list, that it's all over and you have arrived. The trick and possibly the more difficult task is getting everyone in your organization to buy into and implement these systems, and this is where you come in.

Your success or failure will depend on what kind of leader you are and also how big your heart is. I have been very blessed by the beautiful people who have worked for me. Some have let me down and some have done worse than disappoint me. I am grateful to God for first forgiving me, so that forgiveness came a bit easy for me. I have watched employees be able to buy homes because of working for our business, and I have also seen people who have struggled with addiction move on to get married and start their own successful service businesses. So to really be successful in this, you must really care about people and you can't fake it. When you can accomplish that, you will never be the "bad guy."

Stage 4: Mr. Lucky,

As I've shared, when I quit my so-called "great sales job with health insurance and a base salary of $35K plus commission," it was 2008, and I told people I was starting a pressure washing business. Many of my friends and family looked puzzled and asked me if that was "even a thing." But it didn't matter what I was going to do because I knew what I wanted, and what I wanted was the freedom to be my own boss and the freedom to dream. The rest of it came through a lot of grit and sacrifices, trial and error, and even some doubt, but I never quit.

Fast forward three years into Birds Beware and we started doing $50k to $70k a month in revenue, and people began saying, "Awe... he's so lucky. I thought about starting a company like that 20 years ago. I could've done that."

However, remember from my experience, it's not about luck; it's about doing what others aren't willing to do for long enough to be able to have what others can only dream of. The harder and smarter you work, the better your luck!

Remember when I told you about the picture of my family I put on my computer to motivate me and the reward I promised myself? I took that vacation in the middle of the busy season, and we spent 10 days and had a blast. Oddly enough, when we came home, we had more money than when we left! How? I had the systems in place for the business to run without me. I was now an entrepreneur and business owner rather than a self-employed pressure washer. I had, in fact, climbed down the ladder and was making far more money.

I'll close this chapter with a funny story about grabbing what you want:

For as long as I can remember, my father took me and my mother with him to the Optometric Congress in Chicago, IL. We got to stay in the Ambassador East, which is a famous, posh establishment downtown. I loved it, and this being the 70s, children could pretty much run free. The first thing I did upon arrival was to get on the elevator and go to the top floor for the view of the city.

One year, something amazing happened. Like normal, we checked in and once we got settled into the room, of course, I ran to the elevator and up I went. But when I reached the top floor, there were two men there, and they had guns. I thought this was really cool and started to ask them questions, but they didn't answer me because at the same time another man was coming down the hall. The approaching man did all the talking and then asked me my name and why I was there.

I told him all about my amazing mother and father and that my dad was an optometrist. He almost had to interrupt me but asked if I would like a Coke. Now I didn't get sugary treats when I was a kid, let alone a Coke, so I immediately said yes. The man walked me back to his room and when I entered, I couldn't believe how big it was. He got me a Coke and although I don't remember what we chatted about, I do remember that he was very nice, and after I had my Coke, I thanked him and left.

When I got back to our room, I told my parents that I had a Coke with some guy on the top floor, and they were a little mad but got over it. We were going to go out to dinner, so my mother was getting all dolled up, and when we arrived in the hotel lobby, there was a big crowd gathering because someone famous was going to be coming out. So we were waiting and the elevator opened and everyone went wild, including my mother, and I said to her, "That's the man who gave me the Coke."

As he passed us, he waved at me and said, "Hello, Chris."

The man turned out to be Frank Sinatra.

I tell that story because to me it was no big deal but through the years, it has been a fun story to tell, and I liken it to those mountain-top experiences we so long for. ***We live life trying to arrive.*** Now most people in that lobby would have given a lot to have had a Coke with Frank Sinatra, but why?

The reason, I think, is that so many of us settle for mediocrity and in that normal, mediocre life, just to get close to someone famous makes them feel important. I spent a lot of my life wishing I was a famous or important. I have wasted a lot of time wishing I could go back and make better choices, and I wonder that if that were possible, how my life would have turned out.

But the journey of life has brought me to this point, and today I have a decision. It isn't the destination that makes us who we are; it is the journey. Don't look at the wine of other people's lives because the unseen journey of their lives was the crushing of their grapes.

Remember: Nothing grows up at the top of the mountain. The fruit grows in the valley. Embrace your valley and enjoy your walk today because it is all you have.

Working Smarter, Not Harder

- Changing your attitude about money is the first step in growing more of it.
- Without a plan, you can still possibly arrive at where you want to go, but mapping it out ensures faster success.
- First and foremost, you have to understand your "why"!
- You'll need to change your role in order to climb down the ladder of success. Are you a "Lord Joe Saint Stink-o-Lot"?
- Change your shirt, too. You have to stop doing the $12/hour tasks and concentrate on building the foundation needed for your business to operate without you.

- The crew(s) you hire might see you as the "bad guy" sitting in air conditioning while they're sweating on the job. Consider creating transparency about the business, so employees know exactly how they are creating an impact.
- Want to be "Mr. Lucky"? If so, remember this: The harder you work at building your business rather than simply being self-employed the greater your luck will be!

By working smarter rather than harder, you will be more like Clean-Shirt Chris and far less like ol' Stink-a-Lot!

Chapter Four:
Where Do You Want to Go?

Okay… so you're reading this book because you want to make your business better and make your life richer. Perhaps you're realizing that in order for those things to happen, you're also going to have to improve something in yourself.

We touched on mindset in the last chapter and understanding your big "why." Now it's time to fully explore that because without your big "why" clearly defined and really etched in your brain, any advice I share about improving your business isn't really going to work.

So let's start with what might seem like basic questions:

- What do you really want?
- What are you afraid to ask for?
- Do you believe that you're worthy enough for your dreams to be fulfilled… or even exceeded?

Forget about your business right now or the business you're thinking of launching and tell me in one or two sentences what you want out of your life. For some of you reading this book, that might give you real pause because you're so busy keeping your nose to the grindstone that you never bothered to think about it.

Let me re-ask the question in a way that might make it a little easier to answer:

If money was not an issue, what would you be doing today?

I imagine you'll have an easier time answering that since "money is not an issue."

I also imagine that your pushback is that money is indeed an issue. Money is always an issue.

An Embarrassment

I'm going to share an embarrassing story to help me make my point about the importance of knowing – really knowing – what your big "why" is beyond making money.

In 2004, I was really floundering… trying to find myself in business. I had actually been doing a lot of exterior painting. However, I really knew nothing about exterior painting, but I figured it was going to be good because I would be outside and I knew I was not afraid of working hard. So I agreed to paint this lake house, and I really underbid the job. (Anything for *money*, right?) The job lasted… and lasted way too long. I became really tired of painting, so I started drinking again. Around the same time, the neighbor had come over and asked me if I wanted to paint his fence. It was a split rail fence, and I figured I could do it pretty quick, so I told him, "Sure you buy the paint and for hundred bucks I'll do it."

Then reality set in, and I realized that it was going to take me at least two to three days to paint that fence, and when I started realizing I was going to make about 50 bucks a day or less, I just didn't want to do it anymore. So I started to make excuses. But the guy was relentless, and even though I'd given him excuses for three to four weeks, he was still calling me and wanting to know when I was going to come over and paint that fence.

It was at that moment when I reach one of my lows in life. I actually told the guy that the reason I couldn't paint his fence was because I had been diagnosed with cancer. That's how I got out of that job. I was so ashamed. A year later, I saw the guy, and I had to laugh after I saw him because I was in a much better place in my life, so I smiled and said, "Look, it's a miracle!"

At that low point, I was chasing money and the "anything for a buck" mentality, and it took me awhile to realize that money would never be a big enough "why."

Sure I could and did work hard... probably much like you. It's one thing to be relentless at work; however, when you are relentless *and you know your purpose in life*, there is no stopping you!

Drawing Your Dream

Here's an exercise that I want you to do before you go any further. Whether you have clearly defined your big "why" or you are still struggling to put that into words, I want you to sit down with a piece of paper or at your computer and write out how you dream your life will be in five years. This will help you define your purpose and what you want out of your life. You will gain clarity about what may be holding you back from achieving your dream – achieving what you truly want in life.

If you want to skip over this exercise and keep reading instead, I want you to take a few moments to reflect on the *last five* years of your life. Have you been marking time? Have you failed to make any real progress? Have you been so busy working that your life is slipping by?

It's time to really figure out your purpose, and if this book does nothing else but help you define your dream and your big "why," then you win!

I want you to write this exercise from the perspective of your future self-time traveling back to where you are today to tell your current self how things are. Don't give yourself a long laundry list of things to do. Rather, paint a picture of what your life is like – what you want it to be like.

Look, you have a choice today... right now. You can bumble through life and react to whatever comes your way or crosses your path. I did that for many years, and it was a waste of my time. Or, you can choose to be proactive and go after your dreams right now.

> *Stop being reactive to life and start being proactive to reach your goals and dreams.*

If you're out of shape, you have made the decision that exercising and working out is not worth the result. If you are overweight, putting down the donut is not as appealing as being thinner. The whole point of this is to determine whether or not it's worth it. When you start from the present state and all of the things that you are "not," it is going to feel so overwhelming that you will do nothing.

This is why I want you to write to yourself from the future... after you've achieved whatever you are dreaming of!

I recommend you break this down into three areas: health, spiritual, and physical well-being. Where do you want to be? Then look at your family and friends and include a clear assessment of your positives (and negatives) and where you envision yourself in your relationships in three to five years. Also, write about the economic state of your life as you dream it to be in three to five years.

Try not to overthink it but do dream big! I want you to put no limitations on income or money because we can refine those things later.

When you have a vision of where you want to be, then make note of where you are. What are the current positives and negatives about your health and well-being, about your relationships, about your finances? Only with your vision of the future and a clear and honest assessment of where you currently are can you begin to achieve what you want.

I personally find this is a healthy thing to do a couple times a year just to re-assess where I am and my progress toward where I want to be.

Here's a secret: Hard work alone doesn't cut it. The formula to success is:

Current state + written direction + relentlessness and "never stop" attitude = your dreams coming true.

I Got To vs. I Get To

Was this exercise a fun one for you? Dreaming about the future you want? Or did you use this as an opportunity to beat up on yourself? If you have a sheet of paper that includes a lot of "I got to's" (e.g., I've got to lose weight, I've got to make more money, I've got to spend more time with my kids, etc.), I want you to take that piece of paper and burn it or shred it. Literally.

This is your life, and you need to start having more fun with it. You have to start cutting out the "I got to's" and start adding more "I get to's"!

You see, I ended up writing a list of "I got to's," and yes, my list was exactly:

- I got to lose weight.
- I got to make more money.
- I got to spend more time with my family.

And yes, it was very depressing. I was trying to work from my current state, and it was all too overwhelming and seemingly impossible.

Once I understood and used the idea of writing from my time-traveling future self, here's what I ended up with:

"Chris: This is yourself from five years in the future. I want you to listen very carefully because what I am going to tell you is going to change your life. To start with, you will be alive five years from now, so that is great! But more importantly, if you listen to what I tell you, not only will you be living, but you will be killing it as a husband, and as a friend, and as a businessman and entrepreneur.

"So let get started. You are going to become an author, even though you got a D- in English, and people will pay you for your advice on how to grow a service business from the dirt up. Your SAAS (Software as Service) company will take longer than you think to grow, but you will stick with it, and it will be sold five years from now for $100 million dollars. You are going to get to travel and speak at events, and you are going to make a difference in people's lives and businesses.

"Because of this success, you are going to be able to retire at 55 and be able to home school your five children and be able to spend more time with them. In fact, you get to own a giant mobile home and will travel all across America. You will take both of those dream trips you always talk about. You know the ones. In the early spring going from Baja California up to Alaska. And the one in the fall from Maine down to the Florida Keys. Your wife will be so amazed at your leadership skills that she will want to marry you a second time and you will do it. You are going to have a bench seat truck, and just like Bud and Sissy, sit next to each other everywhere you go. You get to grow old with your best friend.

"You finally figure out how to push away from the table before stuffing yourself, and you get to eat more often but you are going to lose 50 pounds and be the same weight you were when you graduated high school. You are going to start running again, and because you get to eat healthier, many of your aches and pains are going to disappear and your skin is going to be radiant. No more eczema. You are going to get to fast for three days every month, and you can't even imagine how good you are going to feel.

"Best of all is that your faith in Jesus is going to explode and studying the Bible will almost be obsolete because you will be living out your faith for the Father's purpose daily. You get to tithe 50 percent of your income, and with the money you make from Send Jim, you will take care of children from all over the world.

"So Chris, get excited: Your life is going to be incredible, and you get to start living it today! Now I really

Where Do You Want to Go?

believe this is going to come true, and because of it, I get out of bed every morning and I work with grit and determination to make these dreams a reality because it is worth it!"

Did you notice all of the "get to's" in that letter? The "get to's" are much more fun than the "got to's." I'm sure you agree, so I want you to focus on your own "get to's"!

> ***There's a big difference between thinking "got to" vs. "get to." The choice is yours.***

If you don't know where you want to go, one thing is certain: you will never get there. You have to clearly define your own big "why" as the first step in building your successful business.

Know the reasons that will motivate you to cultivate your life to win. For me, my big "why" and my faith are intertwined. I see so many out there with their head down and not living out God's plan for us to win. I don't know your faith, but mine tells me that I have been adopted by the King of Kings and that he made me in His own image. That is incredible, and it also means I inherit the whole universe. Now that is worth living for and that makes the hard stuff seem very small. Remember this: "My position is how I am doing (son of the living God). What I do is up to me, and the daily choice is to live out my position."

So many of us are afraid to dream and we're afraid to share our dreams with others because we've been told so many times that we can never have or achieve those things. Stop believing the lies and start believing in yourself. God believes in you and I believe in you!

Stop wishing that your past was somehow different and that you could go back and change things in your life. Those days are over; however, today is a new day, so think of yourself five years from now coming back to give you a pep talk today. Believe it and write it down and relentlessly pursue it, dreaming of your vision daily. The fruit grows in the valley not on the mountain top.

Working Smarter, Not Harder

- The first step toward building the business you want is to clearly understand why you want it.
- Answer this question: "If money was not an issue, what would you be doing today?"
- Money is not a good enough reason to do anything.
- Write to yourself from the future, including exactly how you envision and dream things will be.
- Don't get stuck in the "I got to" mentality. That creates a sense of overwhelm that makes any change seem impossible.
- Instead, focus on what you'll "get to" do when you achieve what you want!

By working smarter rather than harder, you will be more like Clean-Shirt Chris and far less like ol' Stink-a-Lot!

Chapter Five:
Creating the Right Culture

We all have the trick of saying, "If only I were not where I am! If only I had not got the kind of people I have to live with! Why am I surrounded by idiots?"

"If our faith or our religion does not help us in the conditions we are in, we have either a further struggle to go through, or we had better abandon that faith and religion." ~ Oswald Chambers, The Shadow of an Agony, 1178 L

The culture of your organization can easily lead to the ultimate success – or failure – of your enterprise. Company culture does not just happen. It is planned, rehearsed, fed, refined, and most importantly, it's an ongoing process with you and your employees and customers.

Company culture starts with you and the ***investments*** you make in the people who surround you. This area of your life will challenge you the most, and God has a way of bringing us into contact with people who will down right make you want to scream! I think that is done on purpose to show us how we treat Him most of the time. But if we work with the people He brings into our lives, we have the privilege of doing the work of His Son. With that in mind, work with the people around you to build something special in His image. Your tools will be Galatians 5:22-23: *But the fruit of the Spirit is love, joy, peace, forbearance, kindness, goodness, faithfulness, gentleness and self-control. Against such things there is no law.*

Early on with Birds Beware, I had the privilege of making one of our better hires. Because of my background with substance abuse, I could recognize when somebody had come to the end of themselves. Josh had asked me to interview a young woman who had a lot of experience cleaning windows but had been down on her luck for a while, to say the least.

In physical appearance, she'd had all of her front teeth knocked out by an angry boyfriend and had just kicked a heroin addiction; she'd only been clean for six months or so. Because we had established a culture of giving people second chances and believing in their growth and development rather than saying no to what clearly seemed to be – by outward appearance – a bad choice for our company, we said yes instead. And that hire turned out to be the best one I ever made! Through her employment with us, we witnessed this young woman get her life back on track, regain custody of her child, and in the last year of her employment, I had the privilege of being invited to her wedding. Now she owns her own window cleaning company, is married with two dogs, and owns her own home. It gives me chills just thinking about how brave she was and how hard she worked to overcome her adversaries. It really helped me to believe anything is possible.

Take chances on people. I have never regretted helping people even when they burned me. It always seems to be a good gamble, and when things turn out, they typically really turn out well.

Can you recall being hired as an employee early in your career, having been promised things that never panned out, and then you realized that your employer was a fraud?

Chances are your employees are also waiting to find out that you're a fraud. In this current world and in all likelihood, many of them have been burned multiple times by people who promised them the world but delivered very little. So remember this is your game to lose.

This really boils down to excellent communication with the set rules and expectations. You need to clearly communicate where the company is going, what your history has been, and what's in it for the employee.

> *As a side note, my wife and I have fostered 13 children in the past eight years, and it has been messy and hard, and sometimes more than I think I can bear. But we have never regretted saying yes, and God has blessed us with five adopted children when we were unable to have any kids on our own. The story is still going, but I truly believe that in the end, mankind wins when we help each other.*

Hiring Right

Always be recruiting! But I don't want you to simply be looking for warm bodies who can do the work. Instead, always be recruiting a great attitude rather than the skill set! Target the right people, and when you find somebody who might be a fit, put them through an intense interviewing process – one that is automated.

Start with an automated 800-number for them to call if you have to. This needs to be a well-thought-out system. Ask them to follow step-by-step procedures to see if they are capable of following directions. (We go a lot deeper on this at my two-day event, and I have learned employee issues are the number one thing holding small businesses back from real growth. It doesn't have to be this way!)

> *Motivation and attitude trump skill and knowledge every time. Be sure you are hiring for the right attributes. You can teach a motivated employee anything, but it's almost always impossible to change a bad attitude.*

Again, always be looking for people even when you don't need to hire anyone. A lot of the time, that perfect person is waiting on you in a restaurant or changing your oil. Ask great questions, engage in conversations with people, and have the attitude that working at your business is the best and most enjoyable place ever at which to work. Also, find out what their reason for living is – what's their big "why"? Believe it or not, you will meet some really interesting people this way. The very simple but most important key is truly caring about the people around you. If you are rude, a crappy tipper, arrogant, and full of yourself, who is going to want to work for you?

You should have a very clear-cut onboarding process with a complete HR packet followed by strict training. Let them know the history of the company and quiz them on it; let them know where the company is going and where and how they fit in. Clearly define what is in it for them and how will they be rewarded. Under promise here and over deliver. Under promising and over delivering is a good idea for your customers and an equally good idea for your employees.

Each year, Birds Beware shut down for four months out of the year during the winter, and we would let people go on unemployment. As I shared earlier, this normally would start the first week of December, so it was very important for us to throw a memorable Christmas party. If you'll recall, we treated all of our employees and their families to a fantastic weekend at the Bavarian Inn in Frankenmuth, Michigan – complete with five indoor pools and waterslides, indoor putt putt golf, huge game room, and five restaurants. Not only did we pay for accommodations, we also paid for meals and… ready for this? We also gave them spending money!

For the employees, we also had morning meetings during which we mapped out the direction of the company for the following year. We also gave them bonuses at this time and explained very clearly what their opportunity was for the following season. The following spring everyone was on board.

Those two days cost us around $7,000, but it was well worth it because in the following year, the company exploded. Those times at Birds Beware are ones I cherish. Not because it was cool to see everyone's smiles that weekend and not because of the $20,000 check I wrote to myself because I could (although that was pretty cool). And it wasn't when we sold the company at a great profit.

The thing that was most important and that sticks with me to this day was when our first employee bought his first house based on the salary we provided. I cherish those times because I could see people having a chance to improve their lives and have stable income. Plus, at Birds Beware, our employees had jobs in which – not only did they get to work outside – there was no one always watching over their shoulder. We created a culture of trust: Employees knew they could trust us to provide a steady income and deliver on our promises, and we knew we could trust them to get the job done correctly and efficiently.

Trust is a great foundation, and perhaps the only foundation, on which to build your company's culture.

Relationships Are Foundational

Once you have one employee, things change. It's time to start developing close relationships with the people who come into your life. Sometimes you will get gems, and sometimes you will get turds. Now, I hate to call people turds, but let's face it: Sometimes some people are not ready to join the work force.

Don't get me wrong. As you can tell by now, I believe deeply in ministry, but you are running a business. But with that said, like the story about the young woman I shared earlier, really talk to people and understand where they are at in their life. Once you hire them, get to know all that is possible to know about them. Keep a file on everyone – like I explained we'd done in our company. Not a creepy file… but know their kids' names, what their passion in life is, their spouse's or partner's name, what their hobbies are, what type of food they like. This may all seem very trivial, but all these things are very important to understand when you are leading people. It's really simple: people need to be heard, understood, and appreciated. A great leader must be able to listen and empathize.

When most people hear the term or think about company culture, they think it focuses on the inner workings of your business and your employees. However, it is so much more than that! What do you give back to your community? How do you treat your customers when something goes wrong? What do you do when people aren't watching? All of those things contribute to your culture.

We always had a slogan at Birds Beware: "We run toward problems not away from them." That may sound crazy, especially when you are trying to operate a profitable business; however, I really recommend this for anyone. In life when we hide from the unknown, things don't go well, but it is when we embrace our fears and deal with them immediately and directly that we get the breakthrough. I have gotten to the point that even when I know I am only half wrong, I just deal with it, apologize for my part, and move on. Nine out of ten times, it is not that bad.

When I think back on the embarrassing story I shared in the last chapter, I could have just knuckled down and painted that fence in a couple days and collected my money, chalking it up to experience. Instead, I spent as much time coming up with all those excuses and finally making up that I had cancer as I would have painting the fence. As much time (or possibly more) and I had nothing to show for it. Now 20 years later, it's funny to laugh at but really... how pathetic!

There are always going to be problems in your business. How you deal with them and how you correct any mistakes you make is what will set you apart, both in the eyes of your customers and employees.

You Need Cheerleaders

Your company culture is so dependent on how your customers feel about you. And the quickest way to explode your business is to turn those customers into cheerleaders. The only way that you can do this is having a company that:

- Is honest and operates with integrity
- Runs toward problems not away from them
- Cares about their employees
- Gives people second chances
- Has clearly communicated expectations, rewards, and penalties
- And has clearly mapped out the goals and endgame of the company

Remember, you only have to write down your procedures, goals, endgame, etc. once, then it is done! Okay, that's not entirely true because you will want to refine it over time, but the revision and refinement will be easy. Initially getting it on paper is work (I won't kid you about that), but if you want to succeed, it is work you need to do.

So how do we turn our customers into cheerleaders? And at the same time be a scalable business? Early in my days at Phillips Services, I baked cookies for customers. I always did little extra things like that at the end of the job; however, these things were not scalable. And by scalable, I mean that it can be replicated no matter how many customers you add. Obviously, if I tried to bake cookies for all of my customers as I grew, I'd be stuck in the kitchen with no time to do the revenue-producing work!

To create scalability, I recommend automating whenever possible. In the early days of Birds Beware, we hand wrote thank-you cards and that was fine as we were getting started, but by the end of the second year, handwriting 300 thank-you cards each month became a $12-hour job for someone to do.

No matter how small you are now or as you are just getting started, look for automation and strive for scalability because your goal is to grow your company to the point at which these sorts of niceties will be far too time-consuming. You can also outsource. Looking back, I could have paid someone with a baking business to bake cookies for my customers when it became too time-consuming for me.

Communicating clear expectations, attention to detail, building strong relationships, and not being afraid to do what's right even when it hurts or no one is looking are some of the keys to a great company culture. Add to that community, charity, and empathy and you will be on the right road.

It really boils down to just making people feel special and important and to make them feel heard and appreciated. The only way to make a difference in people's lives is spending time with them. This includes your customers, you employees, the people who influence your business, and your friends and family. Get good at this and your life will be blessed.

We don't always choose the people who surround us, but we have a choice to love and care for them. Make the right choice.

Working Smarter, Not Harder

- Your company culture is critical to your success, and it doesn't just happen. You have to build it and continue to nurture it.
- Culture develops from what you do, not from what you say.
- Take chances on people. It doesn't always turn out great, but when it does, it's tremendous.
- Hire for attitude rather than skill. You can always teach a skill!
- Treat your employees right and whatever you happen to spend becomes a true investment.
- Really get to know your employees and take a personal interest in them. It is always time well spent.
- The right company culture will turn your customers into cheerleaders who ultimately drive more business and more revenue and profit for you.

- Do nice things for your customers but work to make those things scalable for future growth.

By working smarter rather than harder, you will be more like Clean-Shirt Chris and far less like ol' Stink-a-Lot!

Chapter Six

Assessment, Action & Attitude

In my teens and 20s, I suffered from the great "Chris Phillips Syndrome." The great Chris Phillips didn't have to have a real job; he could hustle on the streets selling drugs, stealing when he needed things, and could always talk his way out of tough spots.

The sad truth looking back is that I actually believed that crap. Growing up, things came easily for me. I was very athletic, mastered things quickly, and although I felt awkward looking, girls really liked me. I'm 6'3" and my beautiful wife calls me "Dreamy Chris." However, because things came easy, I never learned how to develop the right attitude in life for success.

I despised the valleys of hard work and the daily drudgery of life. I longed for the party; I longed for the mountain top; I longed for the glory; I longed for people to really like me. Basically my attitude sucked!

I was totally self-focused and self-absorbed, and I believed my own lies. But God has a way of humbling the proud... especially the ones he loves... through being really humbled to the point of near death. My attitude truly changed when I died to myself and to the great Chris Phillips.

When your attitude toward life is love and do unto others, we take our focus off ourselves and we delight in others. We even delight in people who are not likable and are hard to be around because we know that's how we used to be. If you take that attitude into business, not only will your customers love you, but your employees will love and respect you as well. Plus it's just a great attitude to have, and you'll start to really enjoy the journey and the mountain-top experiences, and the focus on yourself will diminish as you pour love and time into others.

Plus it is *your* attitude that will forge the company culture of your business. People will follow a leader they can trust.

Assessment

Assessment of your current situation will help you plan out the action steps and systems necessary to achieve your goals. If you do this right, it will actually be extremely time-consuming… but completely worth it!

Assessment is more than just "Am I good?" and "Am I making money?" A solid and useful assessment ends with truly knowing the pulse of your business. If I were to ask you who your competition is in your area, what services they provide, what their pricing is, and what their market share is, I am also going to ask if you've called them and offered to buy them lunch! In buying them lunch, you've offered real value to building a relationship to find common ground with people. While they're your competition, they are not your enemy.

I could write an entire book simply focused on assessment, and I recommend that those of you who have seasonal businesses plan to do a complete assessment over the winter time or your slow season and really go deep. I challenge you to know all the different aspects that are important to your success. (Again, the mastermind class and coaching I offer is ideal to help you with your assessment.)

Consider all these portions of assessing the current state of both your ability as an entrepreneur and your business. The first thing you must do before putting pen to paper is to commit to taking full responsibility for your service business and be willing to do hard things. The point of creating an assessment of your business is to clearly define where you are and to put in writing the purpose of your business and understand where you want it to go.

We cover this in-depth during the three-month mastermind class that I offer throughout the year, but here is an overview of that program that can get you thinking or provide an outline for doing this on you own:

- Document all aspects of your business.
- 25 points of intelligence gathering that you need to know about your business today.
- Climb down the ladder and get out of your business in order to get a bird's eye view of how your company works, current job titles, and where you need improvement.
- Rate yourself as a leader: Are you harder on yourself than those around you? Do you let your team participate in the development of the company? Will you cut out the cancer that occurs in the form of negative attitude, even if it involves family or friends?
- Prepare a written document of your company culture and define your story and plan meetings to share this information.
- Create a plan to deal with uniform issues, dishonesty, bad attitudes, etc. Document your plan and spell out the repercussions

regarding rule breaking, so the person breaking the rules is perceived as the "bad guy" rather than you.

- Define the three operations of your business: sales, service, and operations.
- Begin with the end in mind, so you can work on your business rather than in your business.
- Document your company history and its architecture or organizational chart.
- Carve out and put your dream on paper: How many hours to you work? What is your income? How many employees do you have? How much time do you get to spend with your family and outside of your business?
- Personnel issues: How do you hire and fire? Training your team; employee pay, benefits, and communication.
- Operational issues: Accounting, payroll, and customer relationship management, understanding your assets, phone systems, and software needs. Building a business that can run without your presence.
- Selling: The first call, the estimate, upsells, the second call, scripting for technicians. Selling to large commercial accounts.
- Service: Actually performing the work, organizational skills, and the follow-up procedures.

- Marketing: Direct mail, leveraging the internet, and building a large referral program.

Only when you have addressed each of those issues will you have an honest assessment, and if you skim through that exercise, you are being dishonest with yourself and ultimately short-changing yourself and derailing your chance for your own success. Is it work? You bet it is. (If, having read this list, you want help, please see the Resource section for helpful videos.)

Assessing where you are in your business and in life will prepare you for your next step which is action. Because you now have a written assessment of each aspect of your business, the action will be developing systems to manage these processes. At this point, I recommend an accountability partner.

You need someone who you can bounce ideas off of and someone who is not afraid to tell you when you're wrong or to challenge your thinking. Try to surround yourself with people smarter than you are. This is done by sacrificing your time and efforts to provide real value to these people. Offer to trade your time and services for a small portion of their wisdom.

Changing My Own Attitude

I fully understand the difference that attitude – and commitment – can make in both your life and your business!

In August 1999, my life was over... or so I thought. I had lost my girl, my business, and after walking out of my doctor's office, realized my life was going to end if I didn't get help. So what did I do? I went right to the liquor store and grabbed a half gallon of vodka, went home, and got started ending it all. About half way through the bottle, there came a knock on the door and there was no way I was going to answer it, but to my surprise, the door opened and I thought, "Shit. I didn't lock the door."

In walks my old friend, Betty Walker. I had dated her daughter years back, and she had always been like a mother to me. I remember the tears running down her face as she pleaded with me to get help. After about an hour of the conversation, I decided to go into Teen Challenge, a one-year Christian discipleship program. I was 34 at the time and thought at this point, my life is completely over, but I did surrender... and God blessed me.

However, Teen Challenge was the hardest year of my life. At 90 days, I had lost 60 pounds, was running again, and my mind had cleared. So at the 90-day point, I started squirming and thought that I didn't need this place anymore. I knew if I quit, my family would disown me, but I still pleaded for their blessing to leave. That didn't happen, so I spent the next 90 days just being miserable.

I assure you: This program is no joke. Judges will sometime offer two options when sentencing people: two years in jail or a year at Teen Challenge. It is a free program, but nothing is really free. It was up every morning a 6:00 a.m., Bible study, then work, work, work. That was followed by classes, more work, then bed at 10:00 p.m.

At the six-month mark, I finally thought I had found a way to get out. I am extremely allergic to cats, and the campus cat was always found sleeping in my bed. Well, I had an asthma attack and had to go to the hospital. While I was waiting to see the doctor, my brother showed up unexpectedly and to my surprise, asked me a very simple question, "Chris, did you come here to stop drinking?"

I said, "Well, yes!"

He said, "Let's go get your stuff and get you out of there."

At first I was really excited, thinking, "Finally I can go home and get back my girl, my life, and start a new business."

But then I got really convicted, and I realized that I didn't go there to stop drinking. That was just a symptom of what was going on and what was really going wrong in my life and with my attitude.

No… I went there to get a relationship with Jesus Christ and re-assess my life. Now if you are reading this and are a non-believer, think about this moment in my life when I *finally* got real with myself – when I was brutally honest with myself. True self-reflection is the starting point of change, so whether you serve Jesus Christ or are still contemplating the cross and what it means, know that once I decided to be truly honest, my life changed.

So I didn't use my cat allergy as an excuse to leave and went back with a different attitude. I stopped feeling sorry for myself, and I started to serve and care for others around me who were also struggling. The next six months were still hard, but that time really flew by and my life has never been the same. I still had a lot to learn about business, but it was that moment at the hospital when I truly took an honest look at my life and said, "This time it is going to be different!"

You see up until that point, I quit things when they became hard. I loved to start new things but the moment it wasn't fun anymore, I moved on. I think we all can have success if we stick to something long enough.

Only in looking back at this point can I appreciate how awesome my time at Teen Challenge really was! It gave me enough time to sober up and really re-adjust my attitude and take a good hard look at my life. I think when we look back in retrospect on events and time periods of our lives that are hard, we realize that it was no fun going through them, but these are the moment we cherish the most.

So where are you at today? Have you had that moment in your life when you need things to be different? You, your family, your business deserves you to be totally honest here. Draw the line today, and if you are a Christian, dedicate your plans to the Lord because he tells us that when we do, He will bless them. Make the choice and never quit.

Working Smarter, Not Harder

- You must make an *honest* assessment of where both you and your business are today.
- If you fail to be honest, you are only hurting yourself and your chances to grow your business and create more success for yourself.
- A solid and useful assessment ends with truly knowing the pulse of your business. It

is far more than asking if you're any good at what you do or if you are making money.

- Before you begin your assessment, you must be fully committed and take full responsibility for doing hard things.
- Once you have your assessment complete, it will be easy to evaluate it to determine the action steps you need to take to move your business forward.
- Get an accountability partner!
- I learned the hard way that I needed to be really committed and do the hard work needed. It was the toughest year of my life, but in retrospect, it was also the most awesome one!

By working smarter rather than harder, you will be more like Clean-Shirt Chris and far less like ol' Stink-a-Lot!

Chapter Seven

Setting Selfish Goals

I am one of those guys who loves to be loved. (And I'm probably not alone in that desire!) I go out of my way to make people believe I am "so nice." I want people to say exactly that: "Chris is so nice!" In fact, I have spent most of my life trying to achieve a level of niceness that others would envy.

What a complete waste of time! If I'm really honest with myself, I really want to be a complete bad ass. I want people to be inspired by my life, my walk with Christ, my marriage, and my business. Especially my business! (Now as a Christian, that probably isn't the right order, but this is a book about business, so I am going to roll with it to show you what I mean.)

Why is it that movies like *Braveheart*, *Terminator*, and *Forrest Gump* inspire me? Against all odds, these heroes fight against monsters, villains, and sometimes themselves. The classic story line. Were these heroes afraid if some people didn't like them? No way. (Okay, yeah... Forrest Gump was a really nice guy, but he never gave up on his dream to be with the one he loved.) Or did they run after their dreams with no regrets? That's what inspires me: pursuing dreams with no regrets! Setting a goal and going for it!

It's time to talk about your goals, and I want you to take your goals to very lofty levels. Be selfish here. Yes, I said selfish. Be selfish in your goal setting.

I do love to be loved, but there is also a better way to set and meet your goals than by being a non-confrontational puss… a door mat.

One of the fastest ways men and women sabotage themselves is to think that it's wrong to strongly desire something for themselves that will benefit them and their family. Why is this? I still find myself doing this even as I write this book. My partner, Josh, asked me how I was coming along with the book, and I said, "Good, I am really enjoying the process."

One thing about Josh is that he always asks the hard questions. He holds my feet to the proverbial fire. So he asked his follow-up questions: "How are you going to sell it? Will you just give it away and have some kind of teaching class later like a mastermind? Are you going to do live events?"

My reply: "Well Josh, my goal right now is just to finish the book."

Oops.

Even though he was 250 miles away, I could see his eye twitching!

So he hit me with: "How are you going to profit from that?"

Yes, I do want to profit from my effort. If all you are going to do is write a book without first determining how it will benefit and generate profit for you, then you are likely to have a nice book that people might read and that's it. They'll then put it down and go about their lives, and yes, you wrote a book, but it accomplishes nothing – other than your ability to boast that you wrote a book.

I should have known better... and Josh pointed that out!

Here was my nice, likable goal when I started writing this book:

"I really want to write a book. I think that my story can help people have hope, and heck, if I can build a successful business, then anyone can. So my goal is to write a book by September 2018, and if it's fun and I can make people laugh and somehow inspire them, I think they might even want to pay me to coach them someday."

Pathetic! Time to grow up and do the hard things!

Now that goal sounds all well and good, but what if I were to get over my fear of being too selfish? What if I say what I really want without worrying about whether or not people think my goal is **nice**? What if I allow myself the vision to set a goal that when the book was completed, people would go crazy about how good it was? If I stopped worrying about being too nice or too selfish, wouldn't the goal statement be more like this:

"I will write a book that springs hope and courage to the readers for a better life and will challenge them to build a business that provides massive income with the option to not have to work in their business at all. The book will motivate people to take massive financial action to seek out Chris Phillips's live events and mastermind classes, so they can prosper wildly in their service businesses. And in doing so, it will also make me huge profits. This book will cultivate a fire in the reader to no longer waste time trying things on their own and to completely trust in my method, being convinced that their dreams can happen right now... faster and with less pain!"

Ask yourself which book will be better? The first option gives me an out. It can suck, but hey, at least I wrote something, right? If you are going to set a goal of this nature, I believe you will achieve exactly what you set out to do, and in the case of a "nice, unselfish" goal, your achievement will reflect that: It will be nice and unselfish… and it won't really be very worthwhile.

> *Look at your goals. Are they really worth working toward? Make them big. Make them selfish.*

If your goal is selfish and benefits you greatly in the end, I can bet you that you will make sure to provide your customers (or employees or in my case, readers) with overwhelming inspiration and value. If you fail to provide what you set out to do in your stated goal, you are a phony.

Apply this thinking to your business. Are you a phony? Or are you willing to provide your customers so much value that they can't shut up about you and are raving about you to everyone they know? Are you willing to battle the giants in the land? Are you willing to do what it takes?

Goals Are Self-fulfilling

Let's get back you and your business. Do you find yourself setting goals like, "I want four trucks on the road"? What does that even mean? I understand that goals need to be specific… and measurable… and tangible. There are probably hundreds of books or blogs written on goal setting. If you aren't familiar with the goal-setting process, I suggest you read and research one or two of those.

I agree that goal setting is critical to getting anything done. What I want to do is to inspire and coach you to think bigger… much bigger. Four trucks on the road might be nice and it might be a tangible example of what you really want – a wildly successful business.

Don't be afraid of being selfish about your goals. Your goals should reflect your wildest dreams. Your company's success depends on the selfish, lofty goals you set!

If you are married, did you promise your spouse the things that you *weren't* going to do? Did you stand up and say, "I promise I'm not going to…." Or did you inspire the dream of a life set apart where she was your cherished queen and you were a great noble king, ruler of your lands, a warrior who would fight to the death for her honor? Yeah, that's a lofty goal.

The mind is an amazing thing. While the adage, "If you think it, you can be it," might be incredibly clichéd, it's true. The self-fulfilling prophecy has been studied by countless psychologists. It defines it as, "Any positive or negative expectation about circumstances, events, or people that may affect a person's behavior toward them in a manner that causes those expectations to be fulfilled."

Your belief can come true because you act as if it were already true. Beware: That cuts both ways! If you have negative thoughts and beliefs about what you *cannot* achieve, that is exactly what you are going to get.

The goal you set is the goal you will reach. A goal of four trucks on the road is nice, and if you make that your goal, you'll probably achieve it. Great. So why not make your goal: "Six-figure profit and working half the hours that you do now"? Isn't that what you really want? And yes, you'll have multiple trucks on the road to achieve that.

Don't get me wrong. Simply because you set that goal doesn't make it happen. You have to work hard toward achieving it, but take the first step to put the idea of that lofty goal in your brain. If you don't do that, you will never achieve it!

If you are in business for yourself, you are alone, and no one other than your family cares if you succeed. (Sometimes you don't even get that.) Look, it's not your fault if you don't measure up now. Somewhere along the line being the alpha male or standing up for yourself and going after what you want seems to have gone out of style. It's not "nice." It's "selfish." That's what you've probably been taught. However, I want you to push those thoughts aside and get really selfish about your dreams, ambitions, and aspirations for your business, your family, and your life!

Of course, I am not suggesting that you need to be a jerk about it. There is a balance, and being kind and helpful to others can sometimes be even more of a challenge. But "too nice ain't nice," so don't be afraid of confronting your fears here. In saying this, be very clear: I am by no means suggesting that you act unethically or do anything that goes against your moral standards. What I am saying is that it is quite okay to set a very lofty goal. There is nothing wrong with pursuing success. There is nothing wrong with generating a profit – as big a profit as you can possibly achieve – in your business.

Don't be afraid of confrontation. Start with confronting your own fears and do hard things.

Your service company has a lot of challenges and probably a lot of competition. Don't add to your challenges by being too afraid of confronting your own fears and failing to set a big goal because it wasn't a "nice" thing to do. Don't add to your challenges by allowing negative thoughts drive your own self-fulfilling prophecy.

Yes, I want you to go out and kick the crap out of the competition and make the people who possibly said you would never succeed green with envy. Remember this about lofty goal setting: "If you shoot for the moon and fail, you'll still land among the stars!"

Your Goals

Now that you understand the importance of creating your own positive self-fulfilling prophecy and the need to stop focusing on your own self-limiting beliefs (in fact, refuse to give those any "head space" or mental bandwidth at all!), it's time to set you goal.

Take the time you need right now to write your goals for the next 12 months:

- Where do you want to be one year from now?
- How much will you be making?
- What is your revenue and profit?
- What is happening in your marriage? With your family and friends?

- How many hours will you be working in a year?
- How will you be spending your time away from your business? Hobbies? Travel? Volunteer activities?

When you start with the end in mind, you'll be able to fix that image in your brain and begin working toward it. I want you to write down your 12-month goals that are worth fighting for (like those heroes I mentioned)... and make them amazing... and selfish!

Working Smarter, Not Harder

- First, it's okay to be selfish and dream big. I'm not saying be unethical or immoral, but you're completely allowed to dream big for yourself, your family, and your business.
- Get over your fear about being nice. You can (and must) be ambitious as well as being nice. They aren't mutually exclusive, but worrying too much about your niceness can stifle your success.
- When your goals are selfish, you'll have to do everything it takes to achieve them, or you will quickly be revealed to be a phony.
- The self-fulfilling prophecy tends to be very accurate and works both ways – positive or negative. What you believe usually happens.
- You have enough challenges in your business. Don't "pile on" with negative thoughts and self-talk.

By working smarter rather than harder, you will be more like Clean-Shirt Chris and far less like ol' Stink-a-Lot!

Setting Selfish Goals

Chapter Eight:
Who Are You?

I want to take a few minutes to touch on your underlying mindset, and by that, I mean the one that you probably developed during your childhood. Bear with me while I share what mine was and how it developed.

I can remember a night when I was 5-years-old like it was yesterday. It was a typical hot, humid summer night and I was running around outside. The grass was cool under my feet, and as I rounded the house and stepped onto the driveway, the cool grass went to hot pavement, even though the sun had been down for quite a while (and I was up way past my usual bedtime).

There was a party at our house with many friends and family members there, and an old 70s-style projector played 8mm family films. As I took in the scene and let the pavement warm my cold feet, I suddenly had an appreciation for my parents as a young boy might. I realized they were pretty cool... but that did not guarantee my personal outcome and who I would become. It did not guarantee my mindset.

As I mentioned, my dad was an optometrist, had also started a bank, and had served as a colonel in World War II in the Army Air Corps. My mother was one of the most beautiful women – both inside and out – who ever lived. (Yes, I was biased.) She was also a professional portrait painter who painted portraits of some very famous people, including Michigan Governor George Romney, Roger Penske, and many other GM and Ford executives.

It was a second marriage for my father, and looking back, I believe he regretted not spending more time with his first three children, so he poured into me all the love he could and spent quite a lot of time with me – including twice yearly ski trips to Steamboat Springs, Colorado at Christmas and spring break and regular hiking on Isle Royale National Park, located in Lake Superior.

My father was my super hero, and my mother was the beautiful, nurturing, creative woman who made you feel like you were the only person in the room, if not the world. Yes, I had it good, and I knew it.

But things change in life as they always do, and five years later, my parents were going through a very contentious divorce, fighting about insignificant things like who would own the fine china dishes to far more profound topics like making me choose between them. Then even greater tragedy in my life – my mother was killed in a car accident in 1980, on the very night she'd been commissioned to complete two portraits of the noted cancer researcher, Dr. V., a project that would have easily netted her $40,000 or more.

My mother had also done a portrait of Judge Stephen Roth, whose order for a metropolitan school integration plan in Detroit became a key case on busing before the Supreme Court. I mention that portrait because that one hangs in the Federal Building in Flint, Michigan in the very courtroom in which I was sentenced to 90 days in jail for cocaine possession. In fact, that is the only picture that hangs in that courtroom. In addition to that picture, both of my parents were in attendance.

That day my father told me that if he'd had my talents, he could have been even more successful than he was – even becoming president. He meant well, but it crushed me.

Who's in Control?

Life becomes very precious when we're faced with difficult trials and tribulations, and it's easy to choose to give up and quit. I ended up blaming a lot of my problems on the challenge of following in both of my parent's very successful footsteps, on their divorce, and on my mother's tragic death. I became angry and bitter at the world. I'd had it so good, and it all changed. That attitude was my choice to make.

I believe there are three different spirits or mindsets that you can have instilled in your head in childhood or that you can choose, and I call them the Orphan, the Son (or Daughter), and the Heir.

The Orphan

Do any of these statements or questions sound like you? And be honest; otherwise, you are only fooling yourself!

- I can never find any good employees!
- My competition is out to undercut me.
- Why don't I get any support?
- The economy is bad right now.
- It's not my fault.

If those are comments you make and questions you ask, I believe you have an Orphan spirit.

Consider the child who's truly orphaned. Parents are the ones who meet our needs, but for the orphan, the parents are absent, and the result is that the orphan doesn't (and sometimes can't) trust others to meet their needs. They start to rely solely on themselves, and often go into fight or flight mode due to the stress that too much self-reliance can cause. More often, it turns into flight rather than fight because flight is easier – the path of least resistance.

Those with the Orphan mindset tend to quit or typically skip around from job to job when things get tough. They don't like to follow through; they avoid confrontation; and they blame others for their misfortunes. You know enough about my story to clearly see that I had an Orphan mindset. I blamed everyone except myself for every problem I had.

The blame game is a dangerous place to be because it leads to an inability to forgive, and lack of forgiveness is a two-way street. Many people know the Lord's Prayer, and while they can recite it, even many Christians are unfamiliar with the passage that follows the Lord's Prayer in the Bible (Matthew 6:14-15): *"For if you forgive others for their transgressions, your heavenly Father will also forgive you. But if you do not forgive others, then your Father will not forgive your transgressions."*

Ouch. We sometimes leave that part out.

Answer honestly to assess whether or not you are playing the blame game and embracing an Orphan mindset: "Would you work for yourself? Would you follow you into battle? Would you trust yourself with precious things?"

If you're truly honest and cannot answer "yes" to any of those questions, I'm here to tell you that you're an

Orphan. However, if this is where you are at the moment, it's not too late, nor are you destined to remain an Orphan.

I lived most of my adult life with this attitude and mindset... even after being saved and becoming a Christian. However, with serious attention to my attitude and making different choices, I was able to change it, and so can you.

The Son

The Son spirit knows that he belongs (unlike the Orphan who feels alone), but he questions the rules. In the Son's mind, there are too many rules to follow, so instead, he tends to ignore them, just getting by, and never really grabbing a hold of his own destiny.

Sons can be a lot of fun to hang out with because they tend to misbehave when others aren't looking. Sure, that might be fun for a summer or for a while, but this approach ends without ever really winning but rather always just getting by – never setting any goals and certainly never accomplishing anything.

These are not the type of people you should partner with or take inspiration from. There are a lot of people who are comfortable being the Son.

The story of the prodigal son from the Bible is a great example. He wanted his inheritance "now" and ultimately squandered it. In his subsequent despair, he knew where he still belonged and humbly returned to his father, hoping just to become one of the servants or workers. If you are familiar with the story, you know that instead of returning to be a servant, the father rushes to greet the prodigal son, wrapping him in his robe, giving him his ring, and slaughtering the fatted calf for a celebratory dinner.

As parents, we all want what is best for our children. I'll admit that I'm not shy about wanting my children to win, to do their best, run the race, do the hard thing, take risks, and get up again every time they fall down. I don't want them to quit.

The mindset of the Son spirit is to have others provide for you, but there does come a time when you have to provide for yourself. As much as I know the good I want for my kids, I also know that at some point they'll have to stand on their own.

If you find the Son spirit in yourself, as with the Orphan, it is not too late, and you can change. In fact, you must change if you desire success. You have to do the work. No one else can do it for you.

The Heir

The person with an Heir spirit is the one who truly knows their destiny and understands their place and how to achieve what they want in business and in life. They don't make excuses; they hold to the thought: "If it is to be, it's up to me."

These are the movers and shakers. They're not afraid of failure and embrace an entrepreneurial spirit. They go in early and stay late and do whatever it takes to get the job done! These are the people you want to partner with in business. These are the people you want as mentors. These are the people you want to emulate and ultimately become.

An Heir knows – beyond any shadow of a doubt – that they are loved beyond belief and that their parents want to bless them and that the kingdom is there for the taking!

All three of these spirits have a certain language that they use: The Orphan is a liar; the Son deals in truth; but the Heir speaks in prophecy... forward looking and forward thinking.

If you're reading this, and sitting there recognizing that you have either an Orphan or a Son spirit, you only need to do one thing: You must decide that you want to take your rightful place on this earth, throwing off the shackles of fear, lying, mistrust.

You must decide to become the Heir and take your place on the throne in your business.

It's time to stop making excuses.

It's time to own up.

It's time to do the hard things.

It's time to go out and kick butt.

It's time to claim your kingdom!

Working Smarter, Not Harder

- Despite what may (or may not) happen in childhood, we ultimately all choose our own attitudes and "spirits."
- The Orphan is one who constantly blames others for everything that may go wrong. Their language is that of lies.
- The Son, although speaking truth, relies on others to provide, never setting any goals and never really accomplishing anything.
- The Heir is the one who knows what it takes and gets things done. The Heir speaks prophecy in being forward thinking.

- If you find yourself moving through your life as an Orphan or Son, it is not too late to change… and change you must!

By working smarter rather than harder, you will be more like Clean-Shirt Chris and far less like ol' Stink-a-Lot!

Chapter Nine:
What's Next?

I hope you have enjoyed my story but more than that, my prayer for you is that you take your rightful place as the leader you were meant to be. Run the race set before you with grit and passion, never giving up. The time is now!

I would love to talk with you and understand where you are at in the journey of building your business and life. I love working with inspired people who want to build a legacy... that want to leave an inheritance to their grandchildren.

So what to do next? If you made it this far congratulations!

I currently am the president and co-founder of Send Jim, which is a seven-figure a year SAAS company that is quickly growing to eight figures in the next two years. So while I don't have a ton of time, I am passionate about helping people achieve the freedom that I've been blessed with, so I am committing to work with a select few. *Please schedule a 30-minute, one-on-one call with me to talk about your business and to make sure this is a good fit for both of us. Schedule your call by emailing: chris@thedirtymoneybook.com*

Who I Can Help

Thank you for letting me tell my story, but what about your story? Are you just starting out, have you reached a level of success but feel stuck? Or do you want to explode your business?

If you have you ever wanted to start a service business, I can help.

If you have worked in a home service business and want to start your own business, I can help.

If you have a business and feel stuck, I can really help you!

My super power is helping people grow their business and make more money... by climbing down the proverbial ladder and working less.

Navigating between being self-employed and having your dream business is a difficult journey to try to undertake by yourself. But I know the way because I've already done it, and if it makes sense for you, then let's take that journey together.

I only work with a few people at a time, and I am looking for at least a three- to 12-month commitment. Results are guaranteed or your money back.

I want to tell you about our "Automate, Grow, Sell Bootcamp." How would you like to be trained by the very best in the home service industry? This is a college-level course to super charge your business. Space is limited and there is an interview process to make sure it will work for you.

It will be like a steroid for your business, saving you tons of time from having to read 100+ business books and taking notes to start implementing what they teach by yourself.

It's no secret that the best way to grow is to implement proven strategies and systems from a successful business. I have curated all of my best documents, training, and high-level systems for you to use.

I know you don't want to do it all the hard way. Imagine the power of having everything we are talking about in one single spot. It is all here and organized for you in one place. It's also "go at your own pace" and you have a community of other people to help you along the way. (Find the details in the Resource section at the end of the book.)

As a way of saying "thank you," I want to give you an added bonus! For the last five years, I have talked to thousands of small business owners, and I would love to talk to you.

I'm offering a *free 30-minute consult* to begin helping you climb off the ladder and get started on your journey to success and a great life.

To schedule your call, email me at: chris@thedirtymoneybook.com. In the email, please provide some background on your business and include your website. I look forward to speaking with you soon!

Bonus Chapter:

Blowing Up Your Business: "ChrisP Bombs"

This bonus chapter contains numerous recaps from my assortment of short teaching videos that cover many of the specific tactics you can use that will help you explode your business.

So let's talk to you about blowing up your business. I mean exploding your business so it works when you are not there. I am talking about a business that is an asset that could be sold for six figures or more or could be passed down to your heirs.

Here are a few questions to consider: Why is it that some businesses do more revenue in a month or even a week then others do all year long? Why do some of us struggle living paycheck to paycheck to get by and if we're injured, it's over? How do you go from being self-employed to owning something special that runs without you?

I can tell you from personal experience that it's a lot simpler than you think, and in fact, if you are living paycheck to paycheck, you are actually working longer and harder than the guy with that so-called special business. Look, if you are self-employed, I'm not trying to beat you up and I admit that lived that way for most of my adult life, but something happened to me when I turned 42. I was married and we had our first child, so I started to look at my work, which at that time ran more like a hobby, and I began to wonder what the possibilities were. It was at that point in my life that I took massive action. Here's what I found.

Number 1: You don't have to reinvent the wheel. But you do need to know a few wheel makers. If all your friends and family work for other people, you need to surround yourself with people who have what you want. Here's the great part: you don't have to even know them. You can simply study their systems, online sites, or in books to understand what sets them apart. You also have to take the time to study their methods and apply them to your business.

Number 2: You must determine that the journey is worth the struggle and count the cost. If I told you that for the next year you needed to stop watching the TV, give up all of your fun time (no movies, hunting, fishing, bowling. whatever takes up your time), and sacrifice all of that on the altar of success, would you do it? The answer would probably be no. But if I told you at the end of that year, you would come back to a business that made you $70K a year to start and you only had to work 10 hours or fewer a week... now that's more like it and you'd shout a resounding "Yes!" So count the cost. Make sure it is worth it. I can tell you from experience, having a business that runs without you is worth it.

Number 3: You have to make a radical change from the status quo. I can't tell you how many times I told myself, "This year is going to be different. I am going to get better organized. I will work harder." I, I, I, I. The word repent means to do a complete 180 and walk in the other direction. This will be the hardest thing for you to do because it will feel so unnatural at first. For many of us, it will mean getting out of the truck, off the ladder, putting the squeegee down, and backing away from the truck! Repent from your self-employed ways. This is the only way you can give yourself the time needed to implement the systems of the successful enterprise.

Number 4: Write out the plan or follow one that has already been developed that works, and get yourself an accountability partner, which really loops back into number one in finding a good wheel maker. If you are like me, you will need someone who will be hard on you if you slack off. Someone you can trust who cares enough about you to have the hard talks when things look dark. I recommend paying this person. All the world's greatest achievers pay un-godly amounts of money for personal coaches and mentors, and there is a reason for it. It works.

Angry Customers

Next, I want to talk to you about a subject that is near and dear to me. No, not really dear, but if you own your own business, it is something that everyone has dealt with and will continue to deal with: How to deal with an angry customer.

These people will come to you in varying degrees. You have the passive aggressive. They are the worst because you can sense that something is wrong, but they aren't going to tell you. Instead, they go to the local newspaper or social media and write about what a scumbag you are.

Then you have the yeller. These are my personal favorites because, just like a big dog, their bark is usually worse than their bite.

Next, you have the victim. Ugh. I hate the victim. And last but not least, Satan himself. Sometime you may find that person that is just plain evil!

Angry customers all boil down to fear. Really, the only one of these customers that can hurt you is Satan, and even he has been defeated. (More on that later.) Fear is the worst thing that can happen to you when you get into a situation with a difficult or angry customer. It will make you procrastinate, and worry and imagine all sorts of horrible outcomes that nine out of ten times will never happen.

The passive aggressive (PA) person needs to be dealt with by opening up channels of communication. Sometimes they are hard to detect, but if you find one of your customers acting this way, you need to get them talking. Normally you can figure out where it went wrong if you think back over everything. So you need to bring it up. "Mrs. PA, I'm not sure that we served you at the highest level today, and I sense that we could have done more to exceed your expectations. Can you let me know where we might have gone wrong?" Once you open this can of worms, you need to be prepared to listen for a long time. But just listen. ***Do Not Talk!*** They will tell you how to make it right, and then it's up to you to determine if you want to go down that road. I recommend taking care of them because it is much easier than trying to find a new customer, and most of time, once you go down this road with PA people and solve the issue, they can really become advocates for life.

The yeller. Here's the thing most people who are yellers don't realize – they are coming off like a big fat jerk and normally people get offended and walk away. Not you! Stand your ground. Look them in the eye and let them say their piece. Once they have vented all their anger, you need to do something that works almost every time. You are still looking them in the eye, but you need to remain silent for at least 10 seconds. Then you hit them with this. "Mr. Yeller, I just want to thank you. Did you know that most people wouldn't take the time or the energy to let us know how we could have served you better? I would like to make it right. How can I make this right with you today?" Now if you burned down their house or dropped a ladder on their BMW, well this isn't going to work, so let the lawyer and insurance adjuster deal with it. With yellers, after they yell, they feel relieved or they feel guilty, and after it's over and you stand your ground, you can make a customer for life.

The victim. Let them say their piece, empathize with them, and then take advantage of them again. Just kill them with kindness. Make things right, but victims are going to be the hardest to get them to use you again because it goes against their newest struggle. The best advice I can give you is to run as fast as you can toward your problem. We had a saying, "No problems; just solutions." When you deal with them right away, there is less chance that fear will creep in and paralyze you.

In fighting, one technique is that when you are losing, you grab the person and hold them as close to you as possible. It makes it harder for them to strike solid blows. Do this when dealing with problems, run to it hard and get in close and truly look for ways to solve the situation immediately. If you do, you will build customers for life. Do this all with a great attitude. Even with my new company, I love the challenge to go into battle and win by making it right.

Oh, I almost forgot about Satan, but if you are doing his work, you are going to need more than just advice from me.

Work/Life Balance

Let's talk about balance – your work/family/fun balance.

Admittedly, as I write this, I am out of whack. I am spending way too much time at work. I get in at 9 every day, after I drop off the kids. I have five who are all 8-years-old or younger. Then I am here until 8:00, 9:00… even 11 o'clock, and it is just too much.

There is a reason that God gives us the order that we should live by. We are supposed to put Him first, family second, and work third. But how do you grow a business without putting the work first? It really all boils down to trusting God with your plan.

If you haven't already done this, you need to write down your plans for your business and dedicate it to Him, and then it is His job to bless it. I have really struggled with trusting. In fact, so much of what I do is in my own strength. So this "ChrisP Bomb" is really for me.

Doing things with your own strength will leave you burned out, lost, and in the end, leads to failure for most. I have had many arguments with my wife about all the long hours, and I usually say, "But honey, I am doing this all for you." If I really examine that, it is not true. I am doing it this way because I don't trust God to get me what I think I need. That's the Orphan spirit that I covered in Chapter 8.

My idea for the solution? Just like in Michigan, there are seasons in which we live. And you need to realize that if you are just starting a business, then you are in the dead of winter. This is why you have to have a plan written out. Dedicate that plan to the God of your understanding and trust him.

If you are married or have a family that relies on you, share the plan with them. Explain what you need from everyone; show them the sacrifices and benefits. You are not selling this plan; it simply needs to be a roadmap of what you believe will happen and how everyone fits into it. You need to make sure you put a timeline together and start with the end in mind. If you are only looking to be self-employed, you will endure a very long winter season. I really recommend praying about it.

Having your own business is a beautiful thing, but dedicate your plan to God and he will raise it up. Make sure that the outcome and the struggle are worth it. Have a written plan and timeline, explain how everyone fits in and what their sacrifice and rewards are, and then go for it. Make sure that you do take some time to work on your relationship with your higher power and your family. For winter will turn into spring, and just like in Michigan, after a long winter, spring is a beautiful thing!

Spend Money to Make Money

I want to address the importance of developing relationships with influential people. Let me ask: Would you spend $100 for a new customer? As a window cleaning business, I would pay that all day long because I know that over the next few years that customer is going to produce 1,000 hundred-dollar bills.

So now let me ask: Would you spend $1,000 to get a VIP influencer on board? With Birds Beware, I took the time and spent the money needed to develop relationships with "influencers." I am talking about property maintenance company owners, real estate agents who were killing it, etc. I had one property maintenance guy who produced at least $25,000 every year.

Don't be afraid to spend some money. Offer to take these influential people out to lunch or go to their business and treat everyone to a pizza party every Friday for a month. Make a name for yourself, be generous. Developing any relationship takes time.

I recommend you make a list of the top five people you know who could generate a ton of business for you. Make a folder for each of these people, and then spend the next 30 days putting in the time and effort to get to know them. It is your job to figure out a way to make their lives better.

With property management folks, figure out a way to make them look great to their customers. This could even be offering a few free services to let them know that you have their best interest in mind. One of my contacts for whom I did this didn't give me any work for the first year I pursued him. However, because I was relentless in my follow-up with him, I uncovered a problem that he had. A company that he used to clean the gutters of a very nice condo association had messed up the siding and windows, and it made him look really bad. I jumped at the opportunity to make him look great. I told him, "I can have a crew over there today and we will clean it up for free." That whole thing cost me around $500. But guess who got the gutter cleaning job the next year? We did. That job paid $1,500, and that same year we also pressure washed those condos and did all the outside windows for $10,000. Not a bad payoff for my $500 investment.

One big mistake companies make is that once they get one of these contacts and are doing the work, they stop pursuing the relationship. Big no-no. This is the time to really turn on the charm. The property maintenance company that I just mentioned had 15 dedicated reps who all managed multiple properties. At the end of that one day of free service, coupled with buying them 50 pizzas over the year turned into hundreds of thousands of dollars.

Sadly, that account was lost after we sold the company because no one took the time to continuing to cultivate that friendship. Don't rest on your laurels. Dig deep and solve hard, uncomfortable problems for people, and they will only look to you the next time work needs to be done.

Addiction

This is going to be a bit off topic, but I wanted to talk a little about drug and alcohol addiction. I took my first drink at age 12, and from that point until I was 34 years old, I was controlled by drugs and alcohol. At 19, I got busted with a quarter pound of cocaine, and if it would have happened three months later, I would have done ten years minimum. After doing a 30-day rehab and 90 days in jail as a result, I never did go back to the drugs, but there was my old girlfriend again… alcohol.

In 1999, my life had come to end it seemed. I lost my company, I lost my fiancé, and the doctors gave me less than a year to live. My liver was failing and I was turning orange. I did finally humble myself and decided to do a year in Teen Challenge. Teen Challenge is not only for teens (now they call it Adult & Teen Challenge), but that year was the hardest of my life. You see, I hadn't finished anything of value since graduating high school and my life was a complete lie.

So there I was – 34 years old and going away for one year of my life to get sober or so I thought. After 90 days, I felt amazing and figured, "I don't need this." Many people with drug charges get the offer to do one year in Teen Challenge or do two years in the "can." Many try it for a week or two and opt for the two prison years instead. It was non-stop work, beans, rice, and Jesus Christ. What I didn't realize at the time was that I was dying to myself and my pride. At six months, I really made an attempt to get out and almost succeeded, but it was that day that I came to a turning point in my life.

You see, I thought that I went there to stop drinking, but what I realized that day was that only God could restore me to sanity. I did finish the program and instead of simply quitting the booze, I filled my soul with Jesus Christ. This was a huge thing because, for most of my life, I was an atheist. But the miracles that I witnessed there and the transformation in my own life made me a believer.

I share my story just in case you may be struggling with this issue. If you are, you need to do two things. One, admit you have a problem, and two, fill your life with something bigger than yourself – "The God of your understanding." For me, that was Jesus Christ.

One of the reasons I always worked by myself was because I wanted the ability to take a day off if I was too hung over to work. Plus, a drunk doesn't make a very good employee. But if you are struggling with this and trying to grow a business, I am here to tell you, you can only fake it for so long before you self-destruct.

Don't waste your life telling yourself tomorrow will be different. Take action today and get help. If you need someone to talk to about this, I would love to talk to you. I just ask that you email me at chris@sendjim.com and just say, "Let's talk." All discussion would only be between you and me.

Being a Coach

Have you ever wondered why coaches get paid so much money? And why certain coaches seem to get more out of their player than others? After all, isn't it the player who does all the work? You need to look at this if you want to go from being self-employed to having a real business that runs without you.

Here's another example of the importance of investing in the relationships you have with your employees. If you look closely at certain teams and their coaches, the ones that win the most are the ones that recruit the best and also inspire their players to buy into the team concept. The very best actually inspire their players to the point that they would rather die than lose and let the coach down.

So how do you, Mr. Small Business Owner, learn how to inspire your players? Like all coaches, you come up through the ranks. You have to put in the time starting at the little league level, then maybe coaching a middle school team, then high school, up to college, and maybe if you are good enough, you hit the big time… the pros.

However, many of us want a pro team when we are coaching at a little league level. Most of us will never make college or the pros, but a good "high school coach" can carve out a beautiful business when equating this example to small business. This is the $500,000 to $1 million-dollar business.

I really struggled with this. I am very impatient, and when I'm working trying to get a job done, I'm like, "Get out of the way and let's just get this done." Not a very inspiring approach. If you are like me, you really need to get off the ladder or out of the truck to start to develop your coaching skills. You never see the coach of any team get so frustrated with the players that he puts on a uniform and says, "Get out of the way; I will do it myself." That would be awkward. But let's face it: We do this all the time when it comes to our small business.

How do you develop and hone your skills to become a great coach? It starts by taking an honest assessment of yourself and then your players. If you are the kind of guy who still wants to put on the uniform, then you are going to need to humble yourself and come to terms with the old glory days being over. Take a deep breath and accept that your players are going to fail. Failure is the best teacher. But now, instead of telling them to get out of the way, encourage them.

I know I must sound like a broken record, but you have to really get to know the people who work for you. Know what motivates them and what their dreams and aspirations are. Once you know these things, you can show them how your business can be a vehicle for them to achieve the things they want. You have to be sincere. At Birds Beware, I really did tell people when it was their time to leave and start their own business. Unfortunately, these are normally your best employees and it hurts, but everyone is watching, so if you not genuine in this, everyone will see you for the phony you are.

Be a studier of people and realize we all have our strengths and our weaknesses. Identify people's strengths and team them up with people who complement them. Our best window cleaner was a complete slob. After telling him 1,000 times to clean his truck, I realized it was never going to happen, so I partnered him with my most annual retentive assistant and things worked out. That is your job as an owner. You determine the best players for the best positions.

Success doesn't just happen, and you can wish and hope for a break in the major leagues, but understanding, caring, and mentoring people is the only way to have a shot.

Ownership Joys

I want to talk to you about the sheer joy of owning your own business. Many of us tend to get bogged down in all the responsibilities that come with owning a business. It's like walking the tight rope without a net. No one is going to come to your rescue if you fail… and fall. You will hit the ground with a splat.

However, being the captain of your own ship has a lot of perks. The thing I love most (other the being able to take the day off without having to ask anyone) is having the ability to provide people with employment. I remember when our first employee bought his first house with the income that he made from working for us.

Of course, some employees can give you a lot of headaches. I've heard it said that most people have a least one crisis a week. We had up to 25 employees at one time, so that's a lot of drama! However, when you see what a good paying job can do to boost a person's spirits, there is nothing like that.

In today's workplace, people are feeling disenfranchised. They have heard a lot of promises, and a lot of the time, their employer lets them down... so this is your game to lose. Make sure you under promise and over deliver. Keep a folder on each of your employees. When we sold Birds Beware, one of the best assets we had was the complete folders we had on each employee.

Make sure that you build into their pay several random acts of kindness throughout the year. Obviously, people like money but get them a thoughtful gift as well, something that they will remember more than money to pay off the credit card and other bills. Plan events with all your employees, even when it hurts financially to do so. Build up the story that you have some monster job to do on a Friday, and when everyone gets there, take them to a ball game or something special like that.

Great company moral and company culture just doesn't happen. It is up to you. Remember: This is your game to lose, but if you win here, then dreams can come true.

Answering the Phone

Your phone is hopefully ringing, so I want to talk to you about phone scripts and the importance of having a plan once you get someone on the phone.

For the last five years, I've had the pleasure of calling on over 10,000 home service businesses. Did you know that fewer than 10 percent answer their phone? This is a huge no-no. If you are doing all the work yourself, you need to at least hire an answering service. Think about it. If I'm a woman with tons of money to spend, and I call a window cleaning company to get my windows done and get voice mail, what do I do? That's right – I call the next company listed in the internet search. We caught onto this early with Birds Beware, and it was our goal to already book the job before the competition even called the customer back.

When the phone rings and you answer it, what do you say? How do you get all the important information that you need to produce a new customer? We came up with a couple of scripts to make sure that once someone called, they felt served at a high level and at the same time, we got the information we needed to get the job every time.

Your opening line (intro) should be **unique**. Be different right from the start. Make sure you take a few seconds to explain your process. This really builds perceived value – be a unicorn – and manage the customer's expectations.

The basic data must be gathered in a systematic way. Make sure you get every possible piece of necessary and valuable information. Equally important is having a central place to save all of this data. Use good CRM (customer relationship management) software.

Truly listening to a customer's needs, desires, and fears is critical. Make sure you take great notes and document all relevant information. This step of your script combines basic data gathering, a good CRM, and listening.

The more you can get them to invest in the questions you are asking them, the closer you are to getting the deal!

Typically near the end of a call is a great time to insert "special items." This can change from time to time, but usually include upselling or asking for referrals. Make sure your team is doing this on **every** single phone call.

We have a phone script cookbook that I can send you if you are interested. Just click contact us at chris@sendjim.com

To recap:

- Always answer your phone or get someone who will.
- Explain your process and build value.
- Ask good questions to get the data you need to make the sale.
- Be a good listener.
- Always be upselling, asking for referrals, or offering 10 percent off if they get their neighbor to book the same day.

Paying Salaries

Let's talk about how to pay employees. I can tell you we tried everything: hourly, commission pay as a percentage of the job, etc., and I'll share what we've learned.

When you are starting out and you hire your first employee, I recommend paying them an hourly wage. This person is going to be your assistant, and you will need to make sure right from the start that they understand where the company is going and that they have the biggest opportunity... period. We started a newbie at around $12 an hour. You must also lay out the plan for next season because it is so important to keep good people from one year to the next, so you are not continually retraining.

The next year, your assistant will get their own truck and you will get them an assistant. (A side note: If you do window cleaning and can find a good female window cleaner, do whatever you can to keep her. Most of our clients are women and to be able to send another woman into the house was a huge benefit.)

During the second year is where it gets a bit tricky. I recommend continuing the hourly rate, but you are going to increase the crew leader's rate to around 24 percent of total revenue, and the assistant would get around 14 percent for a total of 38 percent. You really don't want to exceed that number to stay profitable. If your crew can average $100 an hour, then everyone is happy – $24 an hour for the crew leader and $14 an hour for the assistant. This will put pressure on you and your crew when jobs are poorly bid.

At Birds Beware, we tracked these numbers closely and shared the information with the crews. Some companies don't share this detail, but we did. If you do it this way, you will really need to stay out in front of any negativity that can kill your business. If people think they do all the work and they only get a small percentage of revenue, then problems can arise. So you really need to take the time to explain how the growth of your company works and also explain the money spent on sales and marketing.

One you get rolling and you have multiple crews with six figures coming each month, then I recommend a combination of salary and hourly. Salary for the crew leader and hourly for the assistant with the understanding that if they did a great job the first year, then they would get a truck and salary the following year.

Saying No

Sometimes you have to say no to customers who will suck the life out of you, your crews, and will kill your business. I call them spirit suckers!

Do you have a problem saying no? This can be a big problem and can kill your business. Have you ever had a feeling while you were out selling a job that this person was going to be a big problem? It normally goes like this. "Okay Mrs. O., your price for cleaning all your windows and house wash is going to be $1187, and that includes <insert x,y, and z value adds here.>"

There is a pause and she says, "Well, the last company did it for half that."

Red flag! Red flag! Red flag!

Your price is your price. I would handle it this way: "Well Mrs. O., we have standardized pricing and that is what I came up with."

To which she says, "Well that seem like a lot."

Then I would reply with this: "If the other company exceeded your expectations for half the price, why am I even out here?"

Let her answer even if there is a very uncomfortable silence. Don't buy into some jerk's BS of telling you how much you are worth.

If she starts asking how many hours it will take, it's time for you to walk away. Hour counters will want to pay you no more than $30 an hour. At that point, I would usually say, "If you are looking for the lowest price, we are defiantly not the right company for you." You have to be willing to walk away to even have a chance with people like this.

If she says, "I can't find them anymore," you know you have something to work with. "Well Mrs. O., let me explain our company, Birds Beware. Your service will be done by uniformed trained professionals. We only provide the highest level of service. We pay our techs a living wage, and to tell you the truth, I need to charge you enough so that if something goes wrong, like a thunderstorm comes through or a bird poops on your window right after we leave, that I can come back no questions asked with a smile on my face."

Typically, Mrs. O. will come back with a request to handle the job for $800. To which I would reply with a solid "No." Pause. Here's where it gets good if you are willing to stick to your guns.

"Mrs. O., I don't even know if I can get you into the schedule at this point. We are currently running two weeks out and I assumed that you wanted this work done as soon as possible. If you want to wait until August when we really slow down, I can give you 10 percent off. That would bring it down to $1068.30. Would that work for you?"

Sometimes people like this are genuine, and it is just their nature to negotiate with you. But the point I want to make is that you have to stay in control of the conversation, and you have to be willing to walk away from Mrs. O.

Mrs. O. was a real customer and the only one I ever walked off a job on. We worked for her for three seasons on two different properties. The first time I worked for her, I did the job and the result was amazing. But when it came time to pay, she gave me the run around. She finally did pay the full amount two months later. The next year, one of our crew did the work, and she claimed that they broke something so she paid 30 percent less two months later. At that point, we fired her as a customer. The third season, Josh had been running some of the sales leads because our sales guy was out and sold her a $1,500 complete wash at her new home.

When I saw the name, I said, "No way!" But Josh talked me into it and I decided that I needed to do the work myself. Josh's brother-in-law, Tyler went with me. (He is one of the nicest guys your will ever meet.) Halfway through the job, Tyler came out red faced and said, "Chris I can't do it anymore. I am done. I will walk home if I need to." (Thirty miles away, by the way.) She had been nitpicking everything he did. So I went in to talk to her and after about 10 seconds I just said, "STOP. We are done here. What we have done up to this point is free. Please don't ever call us again." I later found out that Tyler had overheard her and her boyfriend talking about how they were screwing the plumber out of $4200 because the Jacuzzi tub was a quarter inch off.

Trust your gut. One bad customer can really mess with your and your crew's attitude. Be willing to say no. Remember you are in control.

Getting Paid

A very important rule in business is: Never make people wait to pay you! What I mean by that is not to discourage your customers from handing over money to you because you don't happen to accept their preferred payment method.

Yes, I fully understand that credit card fees can range from three to five percent, and that those fees can add up. In fact, at SendJim, we spent close to $40,000 last year on credit card processing fees, so I feel the same pain that you do. However, keep in mind that you are providing a luxury service – carpet cleaning, window and house washing, etc. Your customers simply expect you to accept credit cards. Additionally, doing so makes you look like a more firmly established business.

At Birds Beware, we gave all our guys iPads in the beginning and then went on to issue company iPhones. We did so because we wanted to take payment on the day of service, and the easiest way to do it was on the spot... right in the driveway if needed. It worked great, and ultimately we built the cost of credit card fees into our estimate and raised prices accordingly. Sure, we loved when people paid with cash or check; however, when they asked if we accepted American Express, we said, "Yes. We do," with a big grin. Setting up "in the field" credit card processing is pretty easy, and there are plenty of companies that will compete for your business.

Also, when getting paid in the field, suggest that you'll email the receipt. It saves time and best of all, you'll capture the customer's email address for future marketing and to stay in touch with them.

Some companies require a deposit before the work is started. We never did so, and I'll leave that decision up to you. However, I will strongly caution you against running large accounts receivables. It's a quick way to create huge cash flow problems, and it can cripple or destroy your business. Let your customers know in advance that payment is expected the day the work is completed and that you do not send invoices.

Finally, here's one last hint that can make you a ton of money – offer gift cards. Statistics show that almost half of issued gift cards are never used! That number is crazy. It effectively means that you get money up front for work that you will only be required to perform about half the time. Gift card programs are easy to implement, so put one in place now and promote it on every job. For example, "You know, Mrs. Smith, we have a gift card program, and I can save you 20 percent off your bill today for the purchase of a $100 gift card. There is no limit, and if you purchase enough today, your job can be almost free."

Those are a few of the little tricks that will put a smile on your face when you run to the bank!

Roof Cleaning

Let's take a moment to talk about roof cleaning and whether it's the right time to add it to your business along with some techniques on how to get jobs.

With Birds Beware, I constructed our first roof-cleaning rig myself with 35-gallon plastic reservoirs, hose wand, and sure-flow pump. I put it on the back of an old trailer and we were in business. Today, you can buy one ready to go for less than $2,000.

Now roof cleaning is nasty work that can be harmful to your lungs and skin if you aren't careful and will pretty much ruin your clothing. That said, roof cleaning is my favorite job to do. Going out and making $400/hour by myself was amazing, and I could do four jobs a day and still be done by 5:00 p.m. It is no doubt a lucrative venture. How can you assess if this is a service for you to add?

Start by making sure there are plenty of dirty roofs in your area. If you've never cleaned a roof, you've probably never noticed all of the opportunity that may be in your own neighborhood. (Probably not so, if you are in an arid climate.) Start by educating yourself on Gloeocapsa magma... the black stuff that usually appears in streaks. Moss and lichens also grow on roofs and damage shingles.

Once you've educated yourself and established that there is enough opportunity, it's time to educate your potential customers.

(If you've just started a window cleaning or pressure washing business, stick to that service for a year or so and get profitable with that before expanding your service offerings. But keep track of who could use this service.)

Most people don't know that a roof even needs to be cleaned, so you can position yourself as the hero without selling a thing. You're going to educate the community about the problem and then provide answers and solutions to solve it. Start by calling the local paper and suggest doing a story about what may be eating a roof, including what that impact is to insurance coverage. Most companies will not underwrite a homeowner's policy if there is moss growing on the roof. Be the expert about how to actually clean a roof and give them what they need to know about doing it themselves. (Honestly, only one guy ever took me up on suggesting he do it himself!)

You'll close the sale when you explain the cost difference between cleaning and replacement. Be the hero and watch the sales come in.

Accountability

When I was younger, I looked at my business as a vehicle for freedom. I actually started it because I disliked working for someone else. I always hated having to keep to a strict schedule, reporting at 8:00 a.m. and then they owned you until 5:00.

However, that freedom lent itself to laziness. It was very easy to blow off work until tomorrow. Back then, if I were a super hero, I would have been "Captain Tomorrow." Today we are going to party, party, party, and tomorrow we will get serious. With that mindset, it is very hard to get ahead and make a living.

I was 42 before the lightbulb went off and I finally understood that what I was missing was accountability. Thinking back to when I owned Phillips Services, I was married to my young wife and I started to worry about what is going to happen when I get older?

Josh Latimer and I were friends because our wives both worked in ministry for Young Life. I would refer him window cleaning jobs and he would send me pressure washing jobs. We talked about bring the two companies together, but I really didn't want to have a partner. I prayed about the situation, and God told me that He would bless it, but I would have to be second in command. I remember feeling really uneasy about it and almost passed it up, but something told me that I needed accountability in my life. It was the best business decision I ever made. I still owned my own business, but because I had others along with their families relying on me, I really stepped up.

What things do you have in place that hold you accountable? Do you struggle with being a "Captain Tomorrow"? If so, here are a few things you can do. While I really don't recommend partnerships because they are extremely hard and fail often, I do recommend that you find a mentor – someone who has walked the path you are trying to take. Pay this person! The more, the better. When you are paying, you are forced to pay attention. Investing in yourself in this industry is often overlooked, but I can tell you from past experience, it's one of the best ways to grow – and explode – your business.

You can always talk to a friend, but you need to ask tough questions when it comes to friends. Are you the most successful person in that group? If so, you need to surround yourself with people who are achieving at the higher level you want to reach. Self-examination is the starting point of personal growth, so start today and remember tomorrow never comes.

Employee Improvement

Are you scared to let employees represent your company? Are you still doing all the work yourself because you know no one else will do the job like you? Look, you can't grow into a real business and explode its growth until you can trust others to get out there. This was difficult for me. I really struggled with this. I was great at making customers love us and the results we provided, but until I got down from the ladder, I was self-employed – not a business owner or entrepreneur, and I was really only one slip and fall away from disaster.

I've heard other business owners talk about the 70 percent rule in which you can only expect a worker to do 70 percent of the job you do. In my years in business, that sounds about right to me. But what if you only saw a five to 10 percent drop off? Granted, nobody is going to work like the owner and three steps (30%) back won't work... but a half step? I can live with that.

Here's a great technique to make that happen and also get more referrals and positive reviews at the same time. It's an idea that came out of our "Sales and Marketing Super Course."

As I covered previously, Josh and I always made every employee reiterate that we're a small company and depend on and would appreciate referrals and positive reviews. So right before your crew leader starts the job, you make them say, "Mr. Customer, my name is Chris Phillips, and I'm here to do a great job for you and exceed your expectations. If we do, can you do something for me?" Pause. "Referrals and reviews are the lifeblood of our company, so will you provide one when we're done?"

With that, the crew leader is on the hook to do a great job, so you can expect their performance to be almost 95 percent of the great job you would have done if you'd done it yourself. That's how you climb down the ladder of success.

The Art of the Upsell

Wouldn't it be great to be able to double your business this year without paying for advertising? You can and here's one technique to help you achieve that.

When I was growing Birds Beware Window Cleaning, I knew the importance of upselling, so we had a point system for our employees. Each dollar the employee would upsell on a job equaled one point. They had to reach 300 points in a month to qualify and the points could be redeemed for things like movie passes, day trips, gifts for their significant other, etc. We didn't give cash because we didn't think that would mean as much.

We paid our guys really well, especially the team leaders, and we thought this program would be awesome, but to my amazement, the points program was a total flop. So we pushed harder on our guys. You have to upsell and if you want cash instead, you can have cash. But the same thing happened. One guy would do a few... but still a total flop.

As I wondered why this wasn't catching on, I recalled that when I was in the field, the last thing I wanted to do at the end of a job was recommend something else, like gutter cleaning, when I was the one who had to do the work – extending the work day and not getting home by 6:00 as I'd promised my wife. The gutters might get me 200 points, but then my wife and family would be upset. If I, as the owner of the company wouldn't do the upsell, how could I expect an employee to do it?

Lightbulb! The point system was only half of it. The other half came from not forcing the crew to do the upsell work on the same day as the original job. We did pay an additional bonus if they opted to, however. This turned the whole program around, and we even took it further by having crews compete with each other for more upsells with event bigger prizes.

Yes, it cost a little more to drive to a job site to complete the upsell, but it exploded our profits... and I want you to explode your business as well!

Resources:

Get in touch with Chris Phillips:
> chris@thedirtymoneybook.com
> www.sendjim.com
> www.thedirtymoneybook.com

Subscribe to Chris's YouTube Channel to continue getting great "ChrisP Bombs" to explode your business:
> https://www.youtube.com/playlist?list=PLc59RMyftEuFIt YDkOOJgD-8ClFqnTT3m

About the Author

Chris Phillips launched Phillips Services in 2006 and three years later merged with Josh Latimer to grow Bird Beware Window Cleaning and Pressure Washing that they sold in 2015. Chris is currently president and co-founder of SendJim, a software company that helps service companies increase profitablity and explode their efforts. Chris is passionate about business and the service industry and enjoys helping and mentoring new startups in the industry.

Chris lives in Fenton, Michigan and has been married to his one true love for 16 years. Currently the father of six, Chris and his wife, Julie Jo, are foster and adoptive parents to the amazing kids that make up their family.

About the Author

.

www.ingramcontent.com/pod-product-compliance
Lightning Source LLC
Chambersburg PA
CBHW071915200326
41519CB00016B/4624